Contents

page

Acknowledgements

A project of this kind depends upon a great deal of help and co-operation. We wish to express our gratitude to the following people: first, to the headteachers and teachers in the 57 schools who responded to our questionnaires and especially to those in the twelve schools which we visited; second, to the members of the Steering Committee who were a valuable source of professional advice and constructive criticism; third, to Rachel Dixon, who as an M.Ed. student carried out one of the school visits; fourth, to David Satterly for his advice on the analysis of the data; fifth, to Ian Bickerstaff for his assistance with the data analysis; sixth, to NDC colleagues and Dan Duke from the University of Virginia for their support and constructive criticism; and, finally, to Angela Allen, June Collins, Norma Meecham and Joan Moore for their secretarial work on the project.

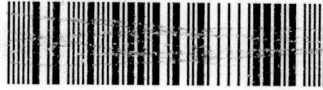

Effective Management in Schools

A report for the Department for Education via the School Management Task Force Professional Working Party

Ray Bolam
University College of Swansea

Agnes McMahon
University of Bristol

Keith Pocklington and Dick Weindling
CREATE Consultants, Cambridge and London

London: HMSO

Department for Education
Sanctuary Buildings
Great Smith Street
London SW1P 3BT
Tel: 071-925 5000

The name of the Department of Education and Science was changed to Department for Education in July 1992. However, the previous name is retained in this publication in references to printed materials issued before the date and elsewhere where necessary in certain other contexts. Some of the professional associations have also changed their titles but are referred to by the name they had at the time of writing.

The opinions expressed in this publication are those of the authors and not necessarily those of the DFE.

Part 1

Introduction

The purpose of this report is to present the main findings of a research project which investigated teachers' and headteachers' perceptions of effective management in primary, secondary and special schools. The project's main aim was:

- to identify management processes and structures in individual schools which staff of these schools have recognised as effective practice.

A second and subsidiary aim was:

- to identify international comparisons, particularly from the United States of America (USA), of management structures and processes which add to our understanding of effective practice.

Background to the research

The background to the project was the Government's educational reform policy, as embodied in the 1986 and 1988 Education Reform Acts. The sheer scale and scope of the changes are worth rehearsing because of their direct relevance to the research. First, the scale of the reform is nation-wide and it, therefore, covers about 25,000 schools and approaching half a million teachers. Second, the reform is a comprehensive one covering virtually all important aspects of school work, including the introduction of a national curriculum; national testing at ages seven, eleven, fourteen and sixteen (ie Key Stages 1, 2, 3 and 4 respectively); local school management with control over budgets, the hiring and firing of staff, school development planning, staff development and buildings; increased powers for parents and community representatives in school governance; compulsory staff appraisal; increased inspection and accountability; open student enrolment and competition between schools for student numbers; and the publication of the school performance league tables based on raw test scores to inform parental choice. Moreover, although some aspects of these reforms are controversial, they are all being implemented, with major consequences for teachers and the management of schools.

As part of its arrangements to support the implementation of this massive and complex series of innovations, the Government set up a School Management Task Force (SMTF) in 1989 to promote the development and training of headteachers and other teachers with school management roles, as indicated in their report *Developing School Management: the Way Forward* (DES, 1990). The Department of Education and Science (now the Department for Education, DFE) has funded this research project on the advice of the SMTF and with the direct support and involvement of the Professional Working Party, a body originally convened by the SMTF which brought together representatives of the national professional associations (AMMA, NAHT, NAIEA, NAS/UWT, NUT, PAT, SEO and SHA), all of which were represented and active on the project's Steering Group (see Appendix 1).

Scope and significance

The following features of the research are worthy of note: first, the project was relatively small scale, with funding sufficient only for approximately 100 days of researcher time; second, it was primarily a descriptive and exploratory study of school management processes; third, the schools in the sample were self-nominated, usually by the headteacher in consultation with staff, as being effectively managed; fourth, it was not a study of effective schools since no independent outcome data were available, indeed the data revealed that the sample included some schools that the staff did not consider well managed; fifth, it does provide systematic, research-based knowledge about the perceived characteristics of effectively managed schools in a context of radical, extensive and national reform; sixth, it is the first British study to operationalise and apply the theoretical and substantive outcomes of relevant British and North American research on effective school management to a relatively large sample of schools drawn from all over England and Wales.

Theoretical framework

The initial perspective adopted in the research arose from the rationale in the SMTF's project specification, which asserted: 'The management of schools is increasingly seen as making a major contribution to the learning and personal development of students. Successful schools do not just happen; they are successful because people make them so and all such people have a stake in management'. This pragmatic stance was developed into a theoretical framework derived from research on effective schools[1], on school management and the implementation of change[2], and on the transformation of school culture[3]. In summary, this framework assumes that, although contingency theory probably offers the best general explanation of effective school management[4], research and experience indicate that British schools perceived by their staffs to be effective are likely to display certain key management features, including :

- strong, purposive leadership by headteachers

- broad agreement and consistency between headteachers and teachers on school goals, values, mission and policy

- headteachers and their deputies working as cohesive management teams

- involvement of teachers in decisions about school goals, values and mission

- a collaborative professional sub-culture

- norms of continuous improvement for staff and students

- a leadership strategy which promotes the maintenance and development of these and related features of the school's culture

- an enhanced capacity to implement the national reforms.

In setting out to survey the views of teachers and headteachers about the characteristics of well-managed schools, the research, therefore, also explored the extent to which these eight broad features existed in the sample of schools.

Research design and methods

With respect to the project's first and main aim, the research method had two components: a postal questionnaire survey and short visits to schools. In response to adverts placed by the six teacher associations in their own journals (see Appendix 2), 57 primary, secondary and special schools throughout England and Wales volunteered to participate.

The questionnaire was designed for the project in the light of the research cited above and was aimed at the headteacher and selected teachers in each school. It consisted of 130 items, mainly of the five-point Likert type, using a scale ranging from 'strongly agree' to 'strongly disagree' (see Appendix 3). These were organised under six headings: school ethos, aims and policy; leadership and management; structure, decision-making and communication; professional working relationships; managing change; the community, governors and the LEA. Most of the items were concerned with process variables (eg, `the head is open to ideas and suggestions from the staff') but a small number were concerned with perceived outcomes (eg, 'academic attainment is high'). Means and standard deviations were calculated separately for primary and secondary respondents in order to compare their overall responses to each item and these are displayed in the tables. The chi square test of significance was used to compare the responses to each item of primary and secondary teachers and these, too, are displayed in the tables as follows: significant differences at the 5% level are indicated by one asterisk (*) and highly significant differences at the 1% level are indicated by two asterisks (**)[5]. Finally, in order to make between school comparisons based on overall staff responses, Z scores were calculated for each school[6].

The main purpose of the school visits was to illuminate, deepen and extend the quantitative findings. Twelve schools were selected on the basis of a sampling frame which included school-type (eg, primary, secondary or special), school size, location (eg, urban/rural), information from the open-ended responses to the questionnaires, and a detailed analysis of certain items from the questionnaires which was carried out as follows. All of the responding schools were compared on fifteen items. Five items were chosen which covered a number of 'perceived outcomes', such as 'academic attainment is high'. The other ten were selected to cover a range of 'perceived process' variables, such as 'the headteacher provides excellent leadership' and 'teachers feel they have a share in major decision-making'. Mean Z-scores were then computed for each school on the fifteen variables and plotted on a quadrant analysis (see Appendix 4). Potential schools to be visited were then chosen from each of the quadrants so that some were relatively high on both perceived output and process items, others were relatively low on both, and some were high on one and low on the other set of variables. The studies of the twelve schools were based on data from the questionnaire responses, on semi-structured interviews (ie, with the head, a sample of teachers and the chair of governors) (see Appendix 6) and on an analysis of school documents.

With respect to the project's second aim, information about school management structures and processes in other countries was gathered mainly through a review of relevant literature. In addition, experts in the field were consulted by telephone, by correspondence and in person, for example, in international conferences, in seminars and during their visits to this country. Some preliminary outcomes of this work were communicated to the Steering Committee at a specially designed day conference in July 1991. The information as a whole has illuminated the work of the project and it is referred to throughout this report in the discussions of the findings. Such information about school management structures and processes in other countries must be read in the context of, for example, the goals of education, the structure of the educational system, the roles and status of school managers and leaders, the methods of allocating finances and resources and the extent to which decision-making powers are held nationally, locally or at site level. Certainly, the differing organisational structures and professional cultures in each country must be borne in mind. For example, in the United Kingdom (UK), headteachers are selected after a process of advertising in the national press and their salary can be, in extreme cases, as much as four times that of a beginning teacher; in Spain, on the other hand, headteachers are normally elected by the teachers in a school from within their own ranks and they receive only a nominal increase in salary for taking on this position; in Switzerland, schools are managed by the local community representatives, there is no headteacher or principal and the teachers are responsible only for teaching[7]. In the USA school principals have traditionally been administrators with no teaching responsibilities but this pattern is now being challenged because of the increased emphasis on instructional leadership and on the restructuring of schools. The reasons for such differences are deeply rooted in the history and traditions of the four countries but the consequence is that their school management structures and processes differ considerably. Accordingly, it is important to make international comparisons with caution.

Description of the sample

Overall, there were 57 schools involved in the project and all were self-nominated. They included 33 primary schools, ranging in size from 56 to 470 students, of all types including nursery/infant, junior, primary and one middle school (9–13). Two special schools taking a variety of students with special educational needs were included in the primary school sample. These schools were drawn from many different LEAs and there was a wide regional spread. 28 of the 33 were nominated by the headteacher and five were nominated by a teacher, after consulting the staff. The 24 secondary schools ranged in size from 580 to 1500 students; one was an all girls school, the rest being mixed; 13 covered the 11–18 age range, one was a sixth form college and the rest covered a variety of age ranges; and there was a wide regional spread. Fifteen of the schools were nominated by the headteacher, nine nominated by another member of staff with the agreement of the headteacher.

Questionnaires were posted to the headteachers and a sample of teachers in these 57 schools. Each primary and special school was sent a headteacher questionnaire and 10 teacher questionnaires, and in many schools this was sufficient to enable every member of staff to respond. Each secondary school was sent a questionnaire for the headteacher and 18 for the teachers. Schools were asked to select a cross-section of staff as respondents taking account of status, gender, length of experience etc. By May 1991, completed questionnaires had been received from 643 teachers and headteachers in these schools, a response rate of 84%. Details of the sample are included in Appendix 5, Tables A1–A5.

By December 1991, visits had been made to 12 of the 57 schools — 7 primary, 4 secondary and 1 special. As indicated above, these 12 schools were selected on the basis of their mean Z-score on 15 of the questionnaire items (five 'outcome' and ten 'process' variables) plotted on a quadrant. Each school was visited by a member of the team who interviewed the headteacher, the chair of the governors and a selection of the staff (Appendix 5, Table A7); these interview data built upon and were supplemented by the questionnaire responses, especially the open-ended comments. Some basic features of the twelve schools are summarised in Appendix 5, Table A6. Additional salient features are as follows:

- **School 1** is an infant school in a small country town with a mixed catchment area and a fairly high proportion of middle class families and transient military families. It scored high on both process and output measures.

- **School 2** is a nursery/ infant school on an urban council estate. The catchment area is working class with a high proportion of unemployed parents, single parent families and 'problem' families. It scored medium high on process and very low on output measures.

- **School 3** is a small junior school in a small market town with a rural, working class catchment area. It scored high on both process and output measures.

- **School 4** is a medium size junior school in a middle class area, with mainly professional parents, on the edge of a large city. It scored medium low on process and medium high on output measures.

- **School 5** is a medium size primary school, with infant and juniors on separate sites, on the edge of a large city with a mixed catchment area of council and private housing. It scored medium low on both process and output measures.

- **School 6** is a large primary school on an urban housing estate, seen by the staff as 'notoriously difficult', and with students who are severely socially deprived. It scored medium high on process and very low on output measures.

- **School 7** is a medium size primary school in a rural/suburban and middle class area. It scored high on process and very high on outcome measures.

- **School 8** is a large 12–18, co-educational, comprehensive school with a socially deprived, urban catchment area. It scored very low on both process and outcome measures.

- **School 9** is a large, 11–18, co-educational, comprehensive school with an industrialised, urban catchment area and students from a range of social backgrounds, but with some who are severely socially deprived. It scored high on process and medium low on output measures.

- **School 10** is a large, voluntary aided, 11–19, co-educational, comprehensive school with an extensive, predominantly rural catchment area with families of all backgrounds. It scored medium high on process and output measures.

- **School 11** is a large, voluntary aided, 11–19, co-educational, comprehensive school with an affluent, rural catchment area. It scored medium low on process and high on output measures.

- **School 12** is a special school with 178 students who have the full range of learning difficulties and come from a large catchment area. It scored medium high on process and output measures.

Outline and limitations of the report

Following this introductory section, the main findings from the project are presented. Some difficulty was experienced in deciding how to do this since many of the findings relate to such broad and all embracing concepts as leadership and culture. It was, however, finally decided to base the presentation on the six section headings in the questionnaire :

- Schools' ethos, aims and policies

- Leadership and management

- Structure, decision-making and communication

- The community, governors and the LEA

- Professional working relationships

- Managing change.

These are followed by two examples, one of a primary school and one of a secondary school, both of which were seen as being well managed. The final section summarises the findings and presents some practical conclusions and implications.

A conventional literature review has not been included in this report. Rather, relevant research findings are referred to in the discussions of the broader significance of the research findings which are presented at the end of each section and in the final section.

Because of the self-selecting nature of the sample, it was expected that the responses would be skewed in a positive direction. This expectation was confirmed: the means for most items were quite high, often averaging about 4 on the 5 point scale, though they were not uniformly high on all items and did vary from school to school. This bias in the sample was built into the project from the outset and its implications must be borne in mind in reading and interpreting the findings. Specifically :

- there is no information about schools which were perceived to be ineffectively managed

- we cannot say how typical or representative this group of schools are of schools in general

- any implications for schools in general must, therefore, be drawn with great caution.

However, precisely because the sample consists mainly of schools which most respondents perceived as being well-managed, it was decided to base the presentation of the findings on the sample as a whole, with any particular differences for primary, secondary and special schools being highlighted as appropriate, and with quotes from particular teachers and schools being included to illustrate and extend these general findings. Finally, two stylistic points should be noted. First, to avoid clumsy wording, the term 'student' is used throughout, but it should be understood to include 'pupils' and 'children'. Second, to preserve the confidentiality of the responses, the gender of the teachers referred to has been altered on a random basis.

1   eg Levine and Lezotte, 1990; Rutter et al, 1979; Mortimore et al, 1988.

2   eg Bolam, 1990; Fullan and Steigelbauer, 1991; Weindling and Earley, 1987.

3   eg Little, 1982; Rosenholtz, 1989; Deal and Peterson, 1990; Leithwood and Jantzi, 1990; Campbell and Southworth, 1990.

4   Hoyle, 1986.

5   A chi square value which is significant at the 5% level (ie $P < 0.5$) indicates that the result could only have occurred by chance 5 times in 100, while a value at the 1% level (ie $P < 0.1$) indicates that it could only have done so once in 100.

6   The Z score technique calculates the mean headteacher and teachers' score for each item in one school and compares it with the mean for the whole sample on that item. This school mean is then divided by the standard deviation (SD), or statistical spread of the scores, in order to convert it into a 'standardised' or Z score. A school with a Z score of 0 can be regarded as having an average score for that item; a school with a Z score of +1.0 has a mean of one SD above the group average for that item; and a school with a Z score of -1.0 has a mean of one SD below the group average for that item.

7   Hopes, 1986.

Part 2
Schools' ethos, aims and policies

The term 'school ethos' is difficult to define precisely. It is used here to refer to the character or tone of an institution and encompasses a number of different characteristics of the school as a workplace. In attempting to understand the ethos of a particular school the questions that come to mind are: What is the place like to work in for students and teachers? What is it aiming to achieve? To what extent do the staff have a shared view about what the school is trying to do? It can be argued that everything that happens in a school affects the overall ethos, and this is something that will be referred to in the various sections in this report. However, the teachers and headteachers in the sample were asked quite directly in the questionnaire what they felt their school offered students, what kind of outcomes it achieved, what the aims of the school were and the extent to which these aims were shared. These questions were explored in more detail in the school visits through interviews with a cross-section of teachers and examination of school documentation. Given that this was a self-nominated sample of effectively managed schools, the researchers were interested in finding out what, if anything, was distinctive about their values and aims. This section of the report focuses on the quantitative and qualitative data about teacher and headteacher perceptions of their school.

Table 1: Teachers' and headteachers' perceptions of school 'ethos'

In this school:	Primary Mean	S.D.	Secondary Mean	S.D.	Significance
Teachers give pupils the confidence to learn	4.39	0.57	4.07	0.63	**
Pupils play an active part in the life of the school	4.33	0.66	3.87	0.91	**
Good pastoral support is provided for pupils	4.32	0.75	4.22	0.87	NS
There is a relaxed but purposeful working atmosphere	4.32	0.77	4.02	0.84	NS
Staff and pupils feel safe and secure	4.30	0.76	3.97	0.81	**
Most pupils feel a sense of achievement	4.24	0.71	3.91	0.76	**
Teachers have high expectations of pupil behaviour	4.13	0.87	3.81	0.87	**
Teachers have high expectations of pupil achievement	3.93	0.96	3.69	0.92	NS
The buildings and grounds are well maintained	3.87	1.04	3.36	1.21	**

In this set of data the mean scores for both primary and secondary teachers were all above 3, and in some instances were much higher. This indicates that the staff agreed or strongly agreed that these were features of their schools. The mean scores from primary staff were higher on all items than from secondary, and these differences were very significant with the exception of three items where they were not significant, (these were 'good pastoral support is provided for pupils', 'teachers have high expectations of pupil achievement', 'there is a relaxed but purposeful working atmosphere'). Given that these scores were all very positive, they do indicate that primary staff on the whole felt, more strongly than their secondary colleagues, that they gave students the confidence to learn, that students were actively involved in the life of the school and that most students felt a sense of achievement. It is unclear why the primary responses were rather more positive but there are a number of possible explanations: for example, the comparatively small size of the primary schools in relation to the secondary schools which might make it easier to establish a whole school approach about how to relate to students or the fact that their students are very young and may be more favourably disposed towards school.

The research did not focus on school effectiveness and no independent objective outcome measures of student performance (eg, public examination results or standard assessment test scores) were available. However, five of the questionnaire items did explore headteachers' and teachers' perceptions of school achievement. These so called 'outcome' measures are suggested as indicators of effectiveness in the literature.

Table 2: Teachers' and headteachers' perceptions of school 'outcomes'

In this school:	Primary Mean	S.D.	Secondary Mean	S.D.	Significance
Vandalism by pupils is not a major cause for concern	4.22	1.07	3.86	1.02	NS
Pupil attendance is consistently high	4.10	0.97	3.71	1.03	**
Discipline is not a major problem	3.72	1.22	3.87	1.05	NS
Most parents are proud that their children attend the school	3.68	0.93	3.94	0.84	*
Academic attainment is high	3.31	1.13	3.62	1.09	**

The mean scores on all five items were above 3 for both primary and secondary teachers, confirming that staff felt their schools were effective in terms of perceived student outcomes. Given the nature of the original sample, this is to be expected. The mean scores from primary and secondary staff for the items on vandalism and discipline were high and the differences between primary and secondary were not significant; for a majority of the staff neither of these factors was a serious problem in their school. The high mean scores for student attendance from both primary and secondary staff indicated that attendance was generally good, though the mean was very significantly higher from the primary phase, suggesting that older students are more likely to stay away from school. On two items the secondary mean was higher than the primary one: 'most parents are proud that their children attend the school', where the difference between primary and secondary was significant, and 'academic attainment is high', where it was highly significant. One hypothesis about why parents might feel a greater sense of pride about their child attending a particular secondary school is that the element of parental choice comes more into play at this stage, primary students being more likely to attend the school nearest their home. The fact that primary staff gave a lower score than their secondary colleagues to the item on academic attainment is rather puzzling given their generally positive orientation (and their responses to the items in Table 3). The explanation may stem from the use of the term 'academic': it is possible that primary teachers associate this with work done at a higher level and with public examinations. However, evidence from the school visits indicates that the percentage of students in a school with learning difficulties and the nature of the catchment area cannot be discounted as explanatory variables. For example, two of the primary schools where teacher responses indicated that discipline was a problem were located in areas of high social deprivation, while schools with a more prosperous catchment area were much less likely to report problems with discipline. These comments from primary teachers help to illustrate this point:

'A sizeable minority of disruptive pupils and pupils with learning difficulties hinders realisation of expectations.'

'The school is in a designated socially deprived area. Consequently we spend a great deal of time as social workers dealing with problems arising in the homes. We aim to encourage the children to develop self-esteem, confidence, and a belief that they have a reason for learning and living.'

and from a secondary school the obverse point:

'The majority of pupils do well because they have strong parental support.'

Teachers and headteachers were also asked what they perceived to be the main aims of their school. Seven of the questionnaire items explored this.

Table 3: Teachers' and headteachers' perceptions of school aims

In this school a main aim is to:	Primary Mean	S.D.	Secondary Mean	S.D.	Significance
Help each child achieve its potential	4.79	0.42	4.43	0.73	NS
Promote the acquisition of basic skills	4.44	0.62	3.95	0.85	**
Promote a spirit of cooperation	4.42	0.64	4.01	0.85	**
Meet personal and social needs	4.35	0.68	4.19	0.82	**
Promote the acquisition of moral values	4.19	0.68	3.81	0.88	**
Achieve good academic results	3.41	1.18	4.02	1.01	**
Promote a spirit of competition	2.26	0.98	2.66	0.99	**

The item, 'to help each child achieve its potential', had the highest overall mean score from both primary and secondary teachers and the first four items had some of the highest mean scores in the whole questionnaire. These are core educational aims and it is not surprising that the respondents felt that their schools espoused them. In the primary sector in particular, there was a cluster of aims which was particularly pronounced: helping each child to achieve its potential; promoting the acquisition of basic skills; meeting personal and social needs and promoting co-operation. The primary mean scores were higher than secondary ones except on two items: achieving good academic results and promoting a spirit of competition. The differences between primary and secondary phases were very significant here, as in the other items in the table. The responses from primary staff were notable in that though they agreed that a main aim in their schools was to promote the acquisition of basic skills, the aim of achieving good academic results was perceived to be less central. This tends to support the hypothesis that they are not comfortable with the use of the term 'academic'.

There was strong agreement from both primary and secondary teachers that a main aim in their schools was to promote a spirit of co-operation, but the item about promoting a spirit of competition had very low mean scores from both groups, though the secondary mean was higher. Teachers appear to have interpreted this question in relation to their work in the classroom with students, and seen it as the opposite of co-operation; because they wanted students to learn to co-operate with each other they frequently placed a lower value on developing their competitive spirit. One hypothesis about why secondary staff placed a slightly higher value on competition is that the external pressures of examinations and the job market increase as the students became older.

A further set of questions explored the extent to which staff felt that the aims and policy of the school were understood and shared.

Table 4: Whether school aims are understood and shared

In this school:	Primary Mean	S.D.	Secondary Mean	S.D.	Significance
Staff are involved in developing the school's aims and policy	4.51	0.58	3.63	0.92	**
Most staff have a shared sense of purpose	4.30	0.72	3.58	0.91	**
There is a concern to build a learning environment for staff as well as pupils	4.28	0.79	3.67	1.03	**
Most staff understand the school's aims and policy	4.26	0.75	3.81	0.78	**
Most staff agree with the aims and policy	4.18	0.76	3.59	0.78	**
Most staff share a common set of educational values	4.14	0.77	3.52	0.88	**
The school development plan is used to review the extent to which aims have been achieved	3.89	0.87	3.50	0.92	**

Again it was notable that the mean scores for both primary and secondary respondents in this set of data were all above 3, indicating that a majority of them felt that, in their schools, staff understood and supported the school aims, and were involved in developing school policy. These are all features which the literature suggests are associated with effective school management. Many, but not all, LEAs now require schools to produce an annual school development plan, and the responses on this item indicated that these are being used as a means of reviewing the extent to which aims have been achieved. However, it was noticeable that higher mean scores were recorded across all items for the primary sector, and that the differences in scores between primary and secondary were very significant. This indicates a greater degree of uniformity and homogeneity in the primary sector, and may result from the smaller size of most primary schools, which can make it easier to establish a shared sense of purpose, in contrast to the greater diversity of secondary schools.

The quantitative data provided a picture of opinion about school ethos across all the schools, and indicated that a majority of the respondents considered that their schools contained many of the features that are associated in the literature with a positive school ethos. This was to be expected, given the sample, but the data also revealed large between-school differences. The qualitative data provided some explanations for these differences in perception.

The school as a workplace

The descriptions given by teachers and headteachers of what their school was like to work in were powerful and illuminating. In the schools which staff had rated highly in terms of process and output measures, the impression conveyed was of a staff working together in harmony and with a sense of purpose, with a student body who, though challenging, did not pose serious problems. A teacher in a primary school in this category said:

> 'It's a good school to work in, with a very good atmosphere among the staff who have a positive attitude and work well together. It's well run and managed. The children are well behaved.'

Teachers also spoke about their schools being happy and relaxed places where they did not feel threatened. This comment was made by an infant teacher:

> 'Nice place to work in; relaxed, well planned and organised; you know what you are doing; you can make mistakes and it does not matter (ie, have the confidence to try things out); I'm very happy here.'

and this from a teacher in a different primary school:

> 'It's rather like an extended family, friendly and caring for all concerned, kids and staff.'

In some of the schools there was an additional dimension of trying to keep at the forefront of change:

> 'Very much in the forefront of things . . .'. 'It's hard because we set high standards'.

A similar comment was made by this secondary teacher:

> 'In some respects it's very challenging because the senior management team lead by example and they like to be at the forefront of educational change; they work very hard but they expect you to work very hard and they set targets of what they expect the staff to do, and that can be quite difficult at times'.

And from another secondary teacher in a different school:

> 'Most staff appreciate the clear sense of purpose emanating from the principal, but are aware of the increased pressure. On balance I enjoy working in this purposeful environment.'

Teachers in several schools were very enthusiastic about working in their school. These comments were made by teachers in the same secondary school:

> 'It's wonderful, very complex but very rewarding'

> 'Superb, very rewarding, satisfying'.

and from a primary teacher:

> 'A place that I love working at . . . the majority of staff are very positive and supportive'.

In contrast, in those schools which the staff had rated less highly in terms of outcome measures, the descriptions of the school as a workplace raised one or other of two factors. The first was the school environment and the problems that the staff felt that this posed for them; the second was when the staff did not feel united or perceived that there was a lack of clarity about the school's central purpose. Teachers in a primary school in a difficult catchment area commented:

> ' - very hard, there are many different demands on you as a person and as a teacher.'

> 'The children are very demanding, it can be quite pressured.'

One of the governors described this school as *'an island in a difficult estate'* and the headteacher's own metaphor for it was, *'an oasis in the desert where children can have time out from the conflict'.*

However, having a more favourable catchment area did not automatically mean that the staff felt good about the school. Two teachers in a primary school where they both reported that the students were well motivated and middle class commented:

> 'It's difficult because it is cramped and noisy. The pressure from parents can be a problem at times and it adds to the stress.'

> 'There is not a lot of direction from the head for me — no staff development'.

Staff perceptions of school ethos were clearly influenced by their view of professional relationships, as these comments from members of a primary school indicate:

> 'There is some friction between the infant and junior staff and the two buildings make communication difficult.'

> 'It's OK, I've been in better and worse.'

> 'It's very stressful for me, I am totally overloaded and need to renegotiate my role with the head'.

And from a secondary teacher:

> 'Easy to agree a set of statements representing a consensus of staff opinion, but the same definition/phrase still means different things to different people . . . individual colleagues have widely differing values and views as to what the school should achieve'.

Perceptions of school effectiveness

As Table 1 shows, the scores recorded by staff across the whole sample were high, which indicates that in general they thought that their school was doing a good job for the students in their care. All the teachers interviewed in the twelve schools thought that they worked in a more or less effective school but, when asked in what respects they thought the school was effective, they did not always find the question easy to answer. The diversity in the responses, even from teachers working in the same school, indicated that they had no common language or set of concepts for describing school effectiveness. Different school features were cited in evidence, the teachers frequently made subjective statements and referred to qualitative but not quantitative data (eg, only one of the primary teachers interviewed referred to the results of Standard Assessment Tests in this context). However, there was evidence that schools which had been visited by one or more members of Her Majesty's Inspectorate (HMI), and had been given positive feedback, subsequently referred to this as an indicator of effectiveness.

The indices of effectiveness that the teachers identified can be roughly grouped into three broad categories:

i   what they felt the school provided for the students;

ii   how the school was perceived in the community;

iii what they thought about the way the school was managed and about the professional relationships between staff.

i   Provision for students — academic and pastoral

The quality of experience that the school provided for its students was a key factor that teachers used to judge its effectiveness. In making their assessment of provision they appeared to measure it against what they felt the students required, given their ability levels and social and personal needs. For instance teachers in two different primary schools — both in socially deprived areas, where poverty was widespread and there were many 'problem' families — gave low scores on the 'outcome' questionnaire items (see Table 2) but clearly perceived what the school did for students to be effective. They spoke about: *'delivering a broad and balanced curriculum, catering to the needs of the type of child that we have; children who can't communicate in a few weeks are asking questions'* and *'the huge range of special things (eg, trips, literary weeks) that were provided'*; also about providing a safe and secure environment for students and helping them to deal with the problems in the home. They recognised that the students might not score highly on standard assessment tests but felt that, given attainment on entry, they achieved a great deal. This is essentially the concept of 'value added', though the teachers generally did not use this term, neither did they have formal ways of assessing student ability on entry to the infant school, so there was no clear bench-mark against which to measure later achievement. There was some evidence that in schools like this the headteacher played an important role in reassuring staff that they were doing a good job. In contrast, staff in another school, which had a much more favourable catchment area and where the staff had recorded high scores on the 'outcome' measures, were the only primary teachers to make reference to hard data:

> 'We were very pleased with the Standard Assessment Tests results; we get good feedback from the secondary school.'

Staff in a similar school, perceived their school to be only medium high in terms of outcome and were critical of their own performance:

> 'Effective for the children but could be better; we don't challenge the above average all the time'.

Staff in a special school felt that effectiveness rested in high quality staff working together for the students and providing a differentiated curriculum for a wide range of students. All this serves to underline the importance of the school context as an influence on teacher perceptions, and indeed, on the whole ethos of the institution. In schools with a poorer catchment area, the staff often used particular criteria, other than test scores, when comparing their progress against that of neighbouring institutions (eg, winning an LEA environmental project, being used as a centre for initial training).

The secondary staff that we have interviewed also saw effectiveness primarily in relation to the curriculum that was provided for students. All four schools were comprehensive, though not necessarily with a fully comprehensive intake, and where concerns were expressed these were often about whether the school's curriculum was sufficiently differentiated to cater for the range of students. Staff in one school, who were confident that the school was effective, indicated that they felt they met the needs of a wide range of students:

> 'It's very effective with a lot of above average but not outstanding students, it's good at pushing them on through; it's usually very good with the most academic and there is a lot of good work as well with very low ability people.'

> 'I think our exam results stand up in terms of LEA figures . . . I think we are particularly effective with the middle ground.'

Staff in a second school were agreed that examination results were good and that the school was undoubtedly effective for the academic student. But concerns expressed by some individuals were that the curriculum was too traditional, insufficiently differentiated and that able students didn't achieve their potential:

> 'Effective within a narrow framework. It's been tailored for the intake and the intake is fairly rarefied'.

Another teacher commented that less academic students 'are not naturally well served'.

One comment from a teacher in a large secondary school which had good examination results, but which, according to several comments, paid insufficient attention to the students' personal development was:

> '. . . this school is primarily an examination factory . . . I feel that pupil development is sacrificed on the altar of academic achievement . . .'.

In contrast, staff in a school which was rated low in terms of student output, spoke of the school being effective in caring for students, but hinted that there was not enough emphasis on academic attainment. The Chair of governors in this school, which was in a deprived area and had a high concentration of 'problem children', spoke of his concern that: *'A recognition of the social problems may well lead to lower expectations of what might be achieved'*. One teacher, echoing this view, attributed this to the high staff turnover leading to inconsistencies in teaching and the innovation mindedness of the management. A colleague in the same school referred to problems in the classroom due to insufficient specialist back-up for students with learning difficulties.

Staff in all twelve schools spoke about the caring, pastoral role of the school as a key component of what they provided for students. The caring role was seen as complementary to the emphasis on teaching and the curriculum, indeed, almost essential to facilitate learning. A primary school teacher said:

> 'Children want to come here; the children are happy and well adjusted socially and emotionally; the children are safe and content'.

In two secondary schools which were rated very highly in terms of process factors, the staff spoke about the quality of relationships that existed between staff and students, as well as about curriculum issues.

> 'It all depends on people. The core of our effectiveness is the ethos, the relationships between members of the school community.'

> 'I think it's effective in helping kids to develop as people, and for kids to feel dignified and valued.'

> 'We are good at building a sense of community in the school.'

ii How the school was perceived in the community

The term 'community' is used here rather loosely to encompass the teachers' perceptions of parental views about the school and also how they felt it was viewed by the LEA. Staff in the primary schools were more likely than their secondary colleagues to refer to parental views about the school as an indicator of effectiveness. If a secondary school was oversubscribed this was referred to, as was the existence of a supportive Parent's Teacher Association (PTA) or parent group. However, the staff did not display the same level of awareness about parental opinion. This may be partly due to the fact that the students were not accompanied by a parent into the school in the morning, as is often the case in primary schools. In interviews, several primary teachers stated that, if the parents appeared to be satisfied, they felt that they were effective. However, it was notable that parental involvement in the school was mainly a feature of those schools with a more favourable catchment area. For example, staff in two schools in this position seemed very conscious of parental views:

> 'the parents feel there is not enough competition and pushing of the brightest';

> 'there are lots of parent appeals to get their children into the school; parents want their children to come here'.

In contrast, in a school in a more difficult area the emphasis was on trying to involve parents.

A second strand to this concept of effectiveness was the impact on staff perceptions of feedback from professionals in the education service (eg, LEA advisers, colleagues in other schools). The deputy headteacher in one primary school said of the school:

> 'The best in the area ... other people measure themselves against us', adding that the school was used as a model for practice (eg, on integrated topic work) for teachers from other schools'.

Staff in one of the secondary schools offered as external indicators of their effectiveness the school's county-wide reputation, the belief that teachers in other schools wanted to work there and the fact that local employers were keen to employ its students.

One primary headteacher was interested in the concept of the 'teaching school'. Student teachers were regularly based there for their initial teaching practice, and the staff were encouraged to engage in consultancy work with other schools in the cluster and to run courses for colleagues inside and outside school. One teacher commented: 'It's almost a training environment'. Senior staff in one of the secondary schools were used as trainers on LEA management courses, and the headteacher of a second secondary school was to be seconded for a year to act as an LEA management development co-ordinator. It is likely that, provided the school did not suffer as a consequence, events like these contributed to a general sense among the staff of the school being effective.

iii School management and professional relationships between staff

The third theme that teachers mentioned when asked about school effectiveness was school management practices and the professional relationships between the staff. In six of the schools staff spoke particularly highly of the management practices. The aspects that appeared to be most valued were: the teachers working together as a team; a clear policy framework within which to work; and opportunities for staff development. These comments from teachers in two different infant schools help to illustrate the point:

> '. . . The way that the staff work together, the way that the staff team feel they can contribute and take part in decision making . . . very well organised, each teacher has a file with all the guidelines, precise instructions, you can find what you want and a good structure makes it easier to do the rest.'

> 'The main strength of the school is the staff, their ability to cope with the type of child, to cope with the type of parent; it's team work, we know at the end of the day we are backing each other up.'

Staff in one secondary school said that relationships were very strong and that they were aware of each others' personal and professional problems and sought to listen, support and give practical assistance wherever possible.

The notion of constantly monitoring what was happening and striving to improve standards was something mentioned in both primary and secondary schools.

'People know what they are doing; they know what high standards are, the aim is to improve those standards, staff conduct themselves professionally.' (*primary teacher*)

'There's constant review and evaluation . . . We are effective in the sense that we know where we're going, getting there and monitoring our progress, we set very high standards with very difficult kids. We are effective, partly because we ask ourselves that all the time.' (*teachers in a secondary school*)

And from a different secondary school:

'I think it is effectively managed, it initiates, it tries to take people along with the initiative, it tries to put in the resourcing that is needed and it is a school that monitors and evaluates itself quite carefully.' (*deputy headteacher*)

'Yes, because we achieve the aims we set . . . ' (*Chair of governors*)

In contrast, in schools where teachers were less satisfied with the management processes, the main complaint seemed to be about the lack of overall co-ordination and structure.

'We have some very good teachers but we need more co-ordination . . .' (*primary teacher*)

'We work well together — the problem is a lack of information and full co-ordination — everyone does their own thing.' (*primary teacher*)

Comments from teachers in one of the secondary schools indicated that they felt that practice in the school resulted in the aims not being met:

'It states lots of aims but undermines most of them by its hidden curriculum.'

'A great deal of paper is wasted in prospectuses, handbooks etc. trying to set out a policy but no serious attempt is made to implement it.'

and from teachers in a different secondary school:

'Following a major restructuring many of the staff are floundering . . . I feel clearer aims and policies need stating and understanding by all staff. Senior staff develop aims and policy but it does not seem to filter down.'

'Academic excellence is sometimes quoted as a priority aim, but the general staff feeling is that every other policy bandwagon has priority.'

Comment

This section has focused on the perceptions of school ethos, aims, values and effectiveness. Teachers in the majority of the schools in the sample perceived that the ethos in their school was generally positive; that discipline, student attendance and vandalism were not major problems; that the school supported what might be termed core educational aims and that staff were broadly committed to some shared goals. These findings are congruent with what we learn from the literature about effective school practices. Mortimore et al (1988) in their study of primary schools concluded that *'a generally positive ethos'* was a characteristic associated with good school outcomes; Nias, Southworth and Yeomans (1989) described a *'culture of collaboration'* in some of the primary schools that they studied which had a beneficial influence on educational practice. The two underlying beliefs of this culture were *'that individuals should be accepted and valued, but that so too should interdependence'*. Rutter et al (1979) in their secondary school study concluded that combined school process factors were strongly associated with student outcome measures and suggested that the process factors might combine *'to create a particular ethos, or set of values, attitudes and behaviours which will become characteristic of the school as a whole'*. Seashore-Louis and Miles (1990), in a study of urban high schools in North America concluded that *'reasonable staff cohesiveness'* was an important precondition for building a shared sense of ownership and a common view or vision about the future direction of the school.

The ethos or culture of the school is made manifest through the pattern of the organisation and the way that people interact with each other. Hoyle (1986) has argued that *'Symbols are a key component of the cultures of all schools'*, and suggests that numerous aspects of the school organisation (eg the roles that teachers hold, the way meetings are run, the documentation that is produced about the school), give out signals about what the place is like and what things are valued. He also suggests that, though all teachers can take symbolic action, the headteacher's role is the most significant one: *'The making of meaning is a particularly important task of the head'*.

Though definitions of what is meant by the term 'school effectiveness' vary it is often understood to refer to student outcomes. It was clear that the teachers in this study had a broader concept of effectiveness. Sergovanni (1991) uses the phrase 'successful schools' and Lightfoot (1983) speaks about 'good schools' and argues: *'I am urging a definition of good schools which sees them as whole, changing and imperfect . . . goodness cannot be measured by a single indicator of success or effectiveness, it is similar to ethos eg, a more holistic notion not the discrete additive elements'*. These perspectives appear closer to the teachers' concept of effectiveness.

The schools in this study as a group were perceived to be effectively managed but there were marked between-school differences in the responses. It was clear from many of the comments made in the questionnaire, and from interviews, that teachers working in schools in socially deprived areas felt that their task was especially hard because of the problems that the students brought with them into the classroom. However, many also indicated that they welcomed the additional challenge that this presented. *'It's never boring . . .' 'It's exciting and challenging to work here.'*

The nature of the catchment area, though a contributory factor, is not a sufficient explanation of why these teachers described their schools so differently, and why their views about the cohesiveness of the school varied so greatly. What were the plus factors that appeared to make the difference? There appeared to be at least three factors that contributed to a more positive school ethos:

- **A clearly stated, understood and shared view** between the senior managers and the staff **about the school's aims and purposes**, in particular what they were trying to offer to the students. Aims which were, in the view of the staff, appropriate for the particular student body, balanced academic and personal and social development and which were implemented and monitored.

- **A supportive, safe working environment** for staff, in which they were not isolated and left to deal alone with any problems that arose but felt confident to experiment and try things out because they knew they could call on the assistance of colleagues if they needed it.

- **A sense of inquiry and investigation, a seeking after excellence which made the school an exciting place in which to work.** This was in no sense change for the sake of change; several teachers commented about the disruption caused when senior managers introduced innovations too quickly and without sufficient planning. Rather, these were schools where there was a clear policy framework, and where existing policies were being effectively implemented but where the senior managers and the staff were in no sense complacent. They were constantly monitoring and questioning the effectiveness of their present practice and considering how it might need to be adapted and developed for the future.

A final point to note is that the teachers appeared to have only limited access to 'hard' data about student achievement and even where available they seemed to make little direct use of it. But they did not have any difficulty in saying whether or not they thought their school was effective and giving reasons for their opinion. However, they were using a broad concept of effectiveness, and their frames of reference and criteria were often particular to their school and thus somewhat subjective, whereas the whole thrust of current Government policy is to introduce performance indicators (eg, scores on national tests, levels of truancy) which are intended to be more objective and universal but which are more narrowly focused and do not take into account the particular circumstances of the school.

Part 3
Leadership and management

At a time when the quality of schooling and the professionalism of teachers are being increasingly challenged, and when teachers are being required to implement numerous externally imposed innovations with little time allowed for each to 'bed in', the wonder is that chaos does not reign in the majority of Britain's schools. That it does not is a testimony to the quality of leadership being provided by headteachers and their senior colleagues and to the professional dedication of the school staff as a whole. In this Part we focus attention upon aspects of leadership and management across the sample of schools, concentrating in particular upon management processes and strategies. We begin by examining whether the headteachers saw themselves as leaders and were seen as such by their colleagues. We look at the contribution of vision to leadership and finally we examine the team approach to leadership.

Leadership and the headteacher

A key finding in the emerging literature on the characteristics of effective schools concerns the central role played by the headteacher. Mortimore et al (1988) referred to *'purposeful leadership'*, where *'the headteacher understood the needs of the school and was involved actively in the school's work without exerting total control over the rest of the staff'*. It was apparent from this and other studies that the traditional autocratic image of the headteacher, managing and ruling by dictat, was no longer viable, although no doubt there are still some who cling to this way of operating. Instead, the image of the effective headteacher is of someone who, in conjunction with senior colleagues, provides a clear sense of direction but otherwise is not afraid to delegate certain management responsibilities and yet is prepared to assert his or her leadership as circumstances warrant. The role is more akin to that of leading and orchestrating a team of staff, striving to harness individual skills and capabilities for the general good. As Duke (1986) has observed, *'Leadership seems to be a gestalt phenomenon; greater than the sum of its parts'*. In formal terms, of course, the headteacher is the leader of the school. However, while some headteachers act as leaders and exercise what we may term 'distinctive' leadership, others either choose not to do so or seem incapable of doing so. Increasingly, attention is being focused on who and what is a leader, and what it is that such persons do. What light does our study cast on this broad area?

Perceptions of the headteacher as leader

Table 5 shows the responses on the questionnaire items which focused on teachers' perceptions of the headteacher as leader and manager.

In general, headteachers in the 33 primary schools were viewed very positively by their staff, as means in excess of 4.0 for 12 of the 15 items indicate. The mean scores on these items for the 24 secondary schools generally were lower, exceeding 4.0 only on one item, and approaching this value only for a further two items. That said however, the fact that mean scores for the sample of secondary schools on 12 of the 15 items were in excess of 3.50 indicates that these headteachers were still rated quite highly by their staff. The result of the chi square test reveals that on virtually every item — 13 out of 15 — a difference that was highly significant was recorded between the phases, confirming that primary teachers agreed more strongly with these items than their secondary counterparts.

Comparing the perceptions of teachers across the two phases throws up a number of similarities as well as some striking contrasts. For the primary schools, the first four items were rated particularly highly. Three of these would appear especially important to primary staff:

- Having the backing of their headteacher

- Enjoying easy access to the headteacher

- Being encouraged to continue to develop professionally.

Table 5: Leadership and the headteacher - practitioners' perceptions

The headteacher:	Primary Mean	S.D.	Secondary Mean	S.D.	Significance
Can be relied on to support teachers in a crisis	4.37	0.87	3.94	1.01	**
Is easily accessible to staff	4.36	0.79	3.91	1.13	**
Often communicates personally with pupils	4.34	0.85	3.84	1.03	**
Strongly promotes staff development activities	4.33	0.72	3.73	1.00	**
Is supported by the staff	4.24	0.77	3.68	0.86	**
Regularly participates in staff development activities	4.24	0.81	3.66	1.06	**
Is regularly seen around school	4.23	0.91	3.39	1.31	**
Is open to other people's ideas and suggestions	4.16	0.86	3.70	1.01	**
Strongly promotes management development activities	4.11	0.84	3.78	0.95	**
Often communicates with staff to express appreciation	4.11	1.02	3.67	1.27	**
Effectively promotes the school in dealings with the community	4.03	0.88	4.14	0.85	NS
Provides a clear sense of direction for staff	4.01	0.91	3.77	1.06	*
Provides excellent leadership for the school	3.98	0.99	3.65	1.09	**
Is directly involved with pupils	3.96	1.08	3.40	1.21	**
Has a structured dialogue with each teacher at least yearly	3.88	1.14	2.71	1.20	**

The first two items were also among the highest scoring items for secondary schools, whilst encouragement of, and support for, professional growth by headteachers was also a prominent feature of the secondary phase. Other elements at both phases had to do with aspects of person management - notably, the headteacher's openness to ideas and opinions voiced by other people, not necessarily senior staff, and appreciation shown toward individual colleagues for outstanding achievement or endeavour.

The only item on which secondary school headteachers were rated more highly by their staff than were their primary school counterparts was in relation to being seen to promote the school effectively within the community, although the difference was not significant.

Few items did not receive strong or very strong agreement in either phase. Only one item stands out in this regard, and only for the secondary sector: namely, holding annually a structured dialogue with staff. (We note however, that in relative terms this was rated quite lowly by staff in the primary schools.) According to the literature on new headteachers (eg. Weindling and Earley, 1987), this would appear to be an exercise which headteachers often undertake on first appointment, but it fails to become routine. For instance, only two of the twelve schools visited featured an annual, formal interview with the headteacher for every member of staff. One was a primary school, the other a secondary. Both headteachers attached high priority to caring professionally for and supporting their staff. Typically, such meetings served several purposes, including: reviewing progress attained; voicing satisfaction and praising or celebrating achievement; identifying areas for future professional growth; and targeting support where it was most needed. At primary level it may be that the value of such a meeting is not fully appreciated given the greater intimacy and contact between headteacher and staff which usually obtains within smaller organisations. At secondary level, while it may be that the task is delegated to someone else, a staff tutor for example, it seems likely that a combination of pressure of work and possibly taken-for-grantedness as headteachers get to know their staff, conspire to erode such activity. With the introduction of a national system of staff appraisal, the extent of regular structured dialogue almost certainly will increase, although at secondary level, the bulk of this work is likely to be carried out by staff other than the headteacher.

Headteachers' approaches to leadership

We turn now to consider what light may be shed on the issue of leadership by our interviews with staff in the twelve schools that we visited. We inquired of headteachers whether they saw themselves as leaders, and if so, in what respects. At the same time we asked their staff whether or not they saw their headteacher as a leader.

It was striking that only seven of the headteachers readily embraced the term 'leader', and few seemed prepared or able to talk about themselves as leaders. Significantly, all twelve headteachers espoused an essentially democratic approach to leadership and management. All of them insisted that they sought to lead in conjunction with colleagues, more especially senior colleagues, this being variously referred to as 'collegial', 'democratic', 'team-oriented', 'open', and 'consultative'. None was autocratic in the traditional sense of management by dictat. All exhibited a genuine concern — manifest in their actions — to consult staff over proposed developments with the objective of building a consensus of opinion. To a greater or lesser extent, these headteachers encouraged staff to come forward with their own ideas and views for strengthening and extending existing practice. All twelve headteachers were distinctly people-oriented — placing emphasis on interpersonal relations and on establishing a co-operative and genial climate in school. That said, some were more effective than others in their ability to manage people, as will become apparent.

The above generalisation does however mask considerable variation among the headteachers as to how they approached the role. Arguably this was most apparent in relation to their prominence in the school and whether they were seen as strong, distinctive leaders. Five of the twelve clearly were influential, even dominant figures in their schools, and although each attached importance to working co-operatively with colleagues, and to delegating, in some cases to a considerable degree, nevertheless there could be no doubting whose voice ultimately counted the most. For example, one primary headteacher was very much the father-figure to a mainly female staff, and although colleagues enjoyed extensive autonomy in relation to curriculum practice and were consulted over school policy, all major policy matters clearly were in line with the headteacher's thinking and wishes. This headteacher declared:

> 'The head is paid to be a leader, to give leadership — but the people have to accept that, and believe in what you're doing...I see myself as a leader, but delegate as much as I can.'

A second, the headteacher of a large secondary school, who acknowledged being a leader — *'You've got to provide fairly clear and definite leadership'* — did so in the context of being the leader of a team of senior managers. It seemed that over the course of some ten years as a headteacher this person had come to recognise the value and significance of leading in conjunction with others:

> 'I think I have learnt how to delegate...as a head you don't have to be a company commander.'

However, though stressing the importance of teamwork, this headteacher volunteered that if the situation demanded he would not hesitate to put himself on the line. Asked to nominate a politician with whom he could identify, he opted for Clement Attlee. The explanation for this choice was revealing.

> 'He was not a magnetic, charismatic figure but could make decisions, could be very firm...I would be worried if I was seen as weak, over-conciliatory, a wet sort of person...I wouldn't describe myself as low key.'

Other attributes which he would not wish to have ascribed to him included being dictatorial, boastful or conceited and inconsiderate:

> 'I hate going back on myself. I would want to be trusted, and to be seen to have integrity.'

The headteacher of another secondary school held similar beliefs about leadership, even though the indications were that the two headteachers differed markedly in the way they managed people. This person was headteacher of a school which bore the hallmark of a particular approach to leadership:

> 'I suppose my style of leadership is best described as consensus orientated: trying to persuade, influence, cajole people where possible...consensus based and giving people a chance to contribute to decision-making. It surprises people when I say, 'This is going to happen because I say so', which you have to do occasionally.... There are times when you have to say, 'I'm paid to make that decision and I will make it and stand by it.'

These and other headteachers who were apparently providing strong leadership were all very clear about the sort of school they wished theirs to be, and about educational outcomes, prominent among which were a concern with standards, excellence — although not narrowly conceived simply in terms of academic attainment — and the quality of human relationships. Furthermore, they were determined to do all in their power to try to ensure that these objectives were widely endorsed by their staff and realised.

Significantly, the views of the staff with whom we consulted in those schools which evidently had strong leaders strongly confirmed their headteachers claims.

'She's in command of everything, she's definitely at the helm.'

'I think she's a good leader because she sorts out what she wants to do, she rallies round the troops...she delegates well, she's informed and enthusiastic, so you trust her, and she's very supportive.'

'One does not mistake who's the head of this school'

and

'He certainly will direct, he doesn't shilly shally.'

(Secondary school teachers)

'She gives direction and vision, but she doesn't lead to the point where no-one else is able to do anything. It's not autocratic leadership but it's not laissez-faire (either)...'

(Deputy headteacher, secondary school)

'I truly think he's quite authoritarian, but he delivers it in a manner that is pleasant ... Although there are loads of staff meetings and management groups, he obviously has the casting vote ... He half makes up his mind, consults and listens and then decides.'

'I think he is quite good at delegating, and he also trusts you to do what he has asked you to do ... Having said that, he still likes his fingers in all his little pies.'

(Teachers, Secondary school)

A whole cluster of teachers' comments from one of the secondary schools provided a graphic portrayal of how things were perceived by the staff.

'She is the major catalyst in school development.'

'She plans and thinks ten years ahead.'

'The headteacher is forceful but not dictatorial — she very much knows what she wants.'

Another group of four headteachers, whose goals were similar to those of the group of five already discussed, employed an approach that was altogether more low-key. For example, the head of a large primary school, whose students were drawn from an economically and socially deprived catchment, was typical in being determined that the school should provide an education of quality, and was keen that it should remain to the forefront of new initiatives. Less typically, this headteacher delegated substantial responsibility to senior staff (these included team leaders), and saw his own role in terms of empowering others, acting as a facilitator and doing all in his power to ensure that staff were capable of fulfilling the responsibilities which they were given.

'I like to lead people to new avenues, (or) to open up an issue.'

He drew an analogy with the internal combustion engine:

'What's the most important thing about a car? It's the engine oil. You're the hardest working part of the machine but no-one ever sees you.'

So, he exercised great care over staff appointments, made a point of assigning newcomers to teaching additional responsibilities once they had found their feet, sought to promote in staff a reflective, critical, questioning attitude to their practice, emphasised the central importance of ongoing professional growth, and made available opportunities for staff to attend courses and to share their professional knowledge and insights with their colleagues through the medium of in-house seminars.

Once again, the views of staff in these particular schools served to confirm the impressions conveyed by the headteachers.

'He is a charismatic head ... a leader who takes people in a certain direction'

and

'One of those people who leads without you realising it.'

(Primary Teachers)

'A good leader — she guides us well. If we are introducing new policies we do it a stage at a time.'

'She leads, but can see when we have had enough'

and

'...she knows what she wants and goes all out to get it. She likes to be thoroughly efficient, and everything is business-like and well-organised'.

(Primary Teachers)

There was however, a small number of instances where the staff view appeared at odds with what the headteacher had espoused. Thus, one headteacher's claim — *'My style of leadership is to lead from the front and by example...(although) I listen to other people's point of view'* — would appear to indicate a self image as a leader, but comments from staff seemed to contradict this. *'The headteacher leaves us to our own devices... There is not a lot of direct input...Sometimes I would like more guidance'*, and *'At times I would look for the headteacher to be a bit firmer'*, were not atypical comments from two members of staff. A second headteacher who clearly aspired to operating in a democratic manner, and who emphasised being non-confrontational and empowering colleagues — *'I want to bring as many people as possible into decision-making'* — in fact was criticised by many colleagues for not being a strong and decisive leader. Six of eight staff interviewed indicated that headteacher could not be said to be an out and out 'leader'. *'I don't think the headteacher has a very high profile'*, stated one. A second observed: '*The headteacher doesn't come over as a forceful leader...someone who you'd have a lot of confidence in*'. '*A bit laissez-faire really*', was the judgement of a third teacher. These views reinforced the earlier impression conveyed by questionnaire responses: '*Consultative management seems to be at the expense of a strong leader... Without a strong leader to pull things together the direction (apropos new initiatives) goes astray.*'

The reverse was the case in another school where there was some indication from the staff that they considered their headteacher to be a leader, even though the headteacher had not claimed this. In a further two schools the view of staff was that whilst each head possessed leadership qualities, neither was perceived to exercise these strongly or sufficiently to act on them. '*The headteacher has a lot of good leadership qualities but does not always apply them, and flits about too much*', was a view expressed about one of the headteachers. A colleague echoed this. '*The headteacher dabbles and doesn't always bring things to a conclusion.*' The deputy headteacher observed, '*should be more positive and decisive as a leader*'. In the second school, the individual concerned, who was new to headship, deliberately had opted for a low-key stance at the outset. This led to staff complaining at the perceived lack of decisiveness. '*The headteacher listens, but that can be a disadvantage*', remarked one. '*We need someone to say, 'That's enough, do it!' 'We need orders sometimes.'* A colleague expanded on this. '*Likes to stand back — he told me he wanted a 'softly softly' approach, but it has been too softly — he should have taken a stand on some issues. He seems to want democracy, but you don't always get a decision.*' A third observed: '*He listens and agrees with everyone, so it's difficult to know what his views are.*'

A further contrast was provided by a headteacher who was heavily criticised by members of staff. This headteacher's goals were in line with the findings from the research literature eg. pupil self-motivation and self-control, and on the experiential approach to learning, teacher autonomy although coupled to exercising responsibility, staff collegiality, yet the atmosphere in the school was characterised by low staff morale and strong dissatisfaction. Clues as to what might have gone wrong were to be found in the comments of teachers. It appeared that the headteacher was not sufficiently in touch with the feeling among staff and had failed to be sufficiently explicit about plans and intentions. This, together with generally poor communication, had led to misunderstandings.

> 'The vision is about (pupil) self-motivation...but it is not appreciated by all the staff and parents, who see a weakness in terms of discipline.'

> 'As a main scale teacher, the outcomes of their senior management team (SMT) decisions don't filter through. There is poor communication. At other times we are consulted on trivial matters.'

Furthermore, the headteacher's way of operating was perceived to be divisive.

> 'It's line management from the top down. There are lots of meetings with the SMT — our 'secret society', as we call them.'

Lastly, and possibly most significant of all, the headteacher was seen to be incapable of acknowledging a different point of view — much less own up to the possibility of having made a mistake.

'She asks for your point of view at staff meetings, then if you disagree she gets very nasty and aggressive...If she is questioned or challenged (or) if she is unsure, she makes you feel stupid.'

'She can't admit she's wrong, and there are lots of upsets in staff meetings but she doesn't smooth it over.'

As already stated, none of the twelve headteachers found it easy or was disposed to talk in much detail about what serving as a leader entailed. Their staff however did not experience any such difficulty, being very clear as to whether their headteacher was or was not a leader and on what grounds. Analysis of their responses has led to the classification below, in which we summarise the qualities, attributes and competences most commonly displayed by those headteachers who were perceived by their colleagues to be effective leaders.

Effective leaders

Personal qualities

- Modelling professionalism eg, behaving with integrity, displaying consistency, being open and honest with colleagues, displaying firmness but fairness in their dealings with staff, hard working, committed, putting concern for students' well-being before personal advancement

- Being well-organised and well-prepared

- Being personable, approachable and accessible

- Displaying enthusiasm and optimism

- Having a positive outlook and striving to act in a constructive manner, rather than being negative and overly critical

- Manifesting confidence and calmness

- Not standing on ceremony or taking advantage of their position; being prepared to help out or take their turn, as necessary.

Managerial qualities

- Formulating a vision for the future development of their school based on personal philosophy, beliefs and values

- Displaying the capacity to think and plan strategically

- Displaying a consultative style of management, with the aim of building consensus and at the same time empowering others. Typically, determining overall direction and strategy, following wide consultation, and then handing over to staff to implement what has been agreed. Effectively delegating responsibility to other people, though following through and requiring accountability

- Ensuring that effective whole school structures are in place

- Behaving forcefully yet not dictatorially. Having the ability to drive things along, yet at the same time displaying sensitivity to staff feelings, circumstances and well-being. Maintaining a good balance of pressure and support

- Being prepared to embrace ultimate responsibility for the school and by manner and actions enabling staff to feel confident and secure

- Displaying decisiveness when the situation demands

- Paying attention to securing the support and commitment of colleagues and enjoying their trust. Actively shaping the ethos and culture of the school and fashioning a sense of community

- Being adept at communicating, and being a good listener as well as keeping people informed

- Being seen to act on information and views deriving from staff, so that consultation was seen to be a meaningful exercise

- Emphasising the central importance of quality in the school's operations and encouraging colleagues to aim high, discouraging complacency

- Ensuring that they kept abreast of new initiatives, though taking care not to be seen to be 'jumping on bandwagons'. Taking steps to prepare staff for future developments, thereby avoiding ad hoc decision-making and crisis management — though being sensitive to the risk of overwhelming colleagues with new practices

- Revealing by their statements and actions that they were in touch with the main events in the everyday life of the school, and that they had their finger on the pulse of the school

- Being proficient at motivating staff eg, by providing encouragement or active support, by acknowledging particular endeavour

- Being able to convey to colleagues that they have their concerns and well-being at heart, and behaving in such a way as to demonstrate this eg, facilitating their development as professionals

- Protecting staff from political wrangling and backing them publicly in any dispute involving external agencies.

Significantly, in spite of the basis on which we obtained our sample, not all headteachers were perceived by colleagues to be effective leaders and managers. Even where teacher perceptions on the whole were positive, it did not necessarily follow that headteachers displayed all-round qualities of leadership. What then were the more common shortcomings of headteachers in their capacity as leaders, as indicated by the teachers' responses?

Ineffective Leaders

Personal qualities

- Lacking dynamism and failing to inspire

- Being insufficiently forceful

- Failing to be at ease with others and to enable them to feel at ease, particularly in difficult and demanding situations

- Inability to accept any form of questioning or perceived criticism.

Managerial qualities

- Being insufficiently decisive. Although most teachers were adamant about the importance of consultation, there came a point where a firm decision needed to be taken

- Either failing to delegate sufficiently or leaving staff too much to their own concerns

- Failing to unite the staff, and to build a sense of a community whose members were all pulling together

- Failing to communicate effectively eg, with respect to their vision, specific objectives or reasons for a particularly contentious decision

- Lacking proficiency in managing fellow professionals eg, being seen to carp at trivialities, behaving in a petty or patronising manner, treating colleagues as if they were children

- Failing to display interest in and concern for staff, or to praise and celebrate their achievements

- Being disorganised and insufficiently thorough, especially as regards administration.

There was one school where both qualitative and quantitative data provided a rather negative portrait of the headteacher's leadership capacity. Much of the staff criticism addressed the interpersonal dimension. For instance, it was claimed that the headteacher became very defensive and even aggressive if challenged publicly, was unable to admit to having been wrong, failed to smooth ruffled feathers or sooth wounded pride, and did not praise staff for their efforts or achievements. Significantly, this headteacher was perceived as not having the concerns of staff at heart. In contrast, arguably two of the most popular headteachers more often than not appeared to get their way, and were very demanding of their colleagues, precisely because staff felt confident that they genuinely cared about and understood them, and could be relied on to support them 100% in any dispute involving anyone outside the school. The following was a typical comment:

> 'An excellent, supportive and well-informed head, demanding of his staff and fiercely loyal to and protective of them'.

Vision and Leadership

The visits to schools provided an opportunity to explore the extent to which headteachers held, and were perceived to hold, a vision to guide the future development of their school. In recent years the concept of 'vision' has been seen as a crucial feature of effective leadership. Possessing a strong vision is said to enable leaders to shape an organisation's culture and, by virtue of their position, they exert a greater influence in this respect than other members. In the context of the present study, vision is taken to mean an image of a possible and desired future state for the organisation which serves to guide growth and development. Of course, simply possessing a vision is not sufficient: leaders need to communicate the vision to colleagues and gain their active support for it. This may entail widening the ownership of the vision, and encouraging colleagues to be stakeholders in the future evolution of the organisation. Ideally, therefore, it should be built with the active participation of colleagues. Further, leaders must act on their vision, for example, by reiterating and reinforcing it or through actions which embody it.

The headteacher's vision

It is against this backdrop that the headteachers of the twelve schools to which visits were made were questioned as to whether they had a vision for their school. In fact each was able to describe some form of vision, which in every case they appeared to have originated. With one exception, there was little indication in the schools that teachers had played a significant part in shaping the vision. The headteachers varied in their capacity to articulate the vision, and the visions were more or less sophisticated. Among the more developed were the following:

'I want this to be the best school in the country - and not just the best special school either. I want an outsider to be able to see the quality of what is happening in teaching and learning. Also, to see that the people who work here are in control of their own lives and responsible for the day-to-day things. There should be high motivation and job satisfaction... . We must be able to demonstrate that this (ie. quality of education) is so...You can't just dream the dream — we need to get evidence of high quality, we need evaluation and feedback. It's not just about human comfort, there must be no lack of a sharp edge in the vision.'

'Somewhere where staff and children all feel that they are having the greatest opportunity to make the most of themselves — in the very widest sense. Where they feel valued and can grow... . A comprehensive school with the highest standards, and expectations of real achievement for everyone...'

and

'A centre of excellence at the heart of the community.'

'My vision is of a good primary school; getting good academic attainment through good teaching and discipline, where children are hard working and are happy.'

It was apparent that the headteachers' visions were not static but were dynamic and flexible, and were modified to take account of changing circumstances.

As indicated below, there was a great deal of commonality in the components of the different visions which headteachers outlined for us.

- To challenge all students, to encourage each to realise his/her potential; to encourage hard work and application

- To implement teaching and learning of quality; simply providing a caring environment was not sufficient

- To create a happy environment; further, one in which students would feel safe and secure

- To foster staff autonomy, enabling them to exercise greater control over their professional working lives — though at the same time assuming responsibility, both for self and others

- To praise teachers for their achievements and/or application, and to make them feel valued

- To afford parents/the wider community respect, and to attend to their needs and concerns

- To foster greater co-operation between staff and to build sound teamwork

- To respect other people — students as well as staff

- To create an environment which was stimulating both for staff and students

- To instil sound student discipline

- To establish an effective system for monitoring school practice.

Although primary and secondary headteachers shared much in common, there were, of course, certain differences, mainly related to the curriculum. There was, for example, reference to the need to develop the creative and expressive arts in one secondary school, and in another, of the need for greater diversification at sixth form level. In a third school, organisational aspects were alluded to eg, the need to reorganise the school into smaller units with which both students and staff might identify.

Not surprisingly, every headteacher made mention of the education provided for students. Some were content to state that they wished each child to realise his/her potential eg, 'valuing the students for what they are worth and trying to achieve' — an uncontentious statement of intent. Others went further however, touching on the potentially thorny issues of expectations, quality and standards in such comments as:

- getting good academic attainment through good teaching and discipline

- 'to aim for the highest standard that any child can achieve... to push quality as far down the system as possible'

- 'a school with the highest standards and expectations of real achievement for everyone'.

It was notable that staff were explicitly referred to by seven of the twelve headteachers. Typically, comments gave a clue as to the nature of the work environment. The most explicit outlined the following aims:

- to trust in teachers as professionals, to accord them autonomy

- to encourage self-management and to urge joint responsibility

- to emphasise teamwork, fostering close co-operation and, where possible, active collaboration.

Another headteacher made specific reference to developing the management capabilities of staff — and not just senior colleagues. The school had its own in-house training provision for middle as well as senior managers. In addition, the headteacher looked favourably on changes of role as a means of enhancing colleagues' capabilities.

In general, the components of the vision which most of the headteachers described would seem neither surprising nor striking nor controversial. They are closely in line with what one might expect of the British system of education. However, the vision of one headteacher introduced some novel elements:

- The notion of the school as a sort of 'test track' for experimenting with new ideas and practices

- The desire for the school to play a more substantial role than hitherto in the training of new recruits to the profession — the concept of the 'teaching' or 'laboratory' school

- The wish for the school to serve as a focal point of the community — in this instance, characterised by pronounced deprivation. This might embrace a whole range of functions eg. social centre, information resource, a source of adult learning provision.

The source of the vision

Headteachers were asked about the origins of their vision. Invariably, there were references to one or more individuals whom they had encountered earlier in their careers, and whose thinking and practice clearly had made a profound impression. The four headteachers who were best able to articulate a well developed vision had read widely, and not just the literature on management, might be described as 'thinkers', and tended to have an involvement in educational practices which extended beyond the boundaries of their respective schools eg, tutoring on in-service courses, sitting on LEA or professional association committees and working parties. They gave every indication of having debated at length educational values and issues, of having engaged critically with the relevant literature, and of having worked out for themselves a basic philosophy of education to which they subscribed — their 'educational platform' — and which actively informed their actions as leaders of schools. One explained:

'The vision grew out of my experience, and it keeps developing. It's about me and my approach to life first of all. It's about how people relate to each other, both inside and outside schools'.

A second observed:

> 'It's very much a personal philosophy, what you want in education. I always try to assess what I want as an educationalist and as a parent. It's also arrived at by talking to colleagues and by external views, HMI for example, who have indicated to us that we should try to keep what we have in the school in terms of relationships which is quite special. But you are also influenced in your vision by taking a realistic view of what the weaknesses are at present. I think the key to any good management is to avoid complacency in areas of (present) strength and be realistic about areas that need major development.'

Significantly, save in one instance, there was little indication in any of the schools of teachers having played a part in shaping the vision. The exception was a secondary school where much effort went into building a distinct sense of a shared vision which was not fixed for all time but could be modified in line with changing circumstances. It was reviewed collectively on a regular basis. As one member of staff remarked, *'There is a real sense of belonging and of shared purpose and values'*.

Staff understanding of the vision

Members of staff were asked about their headteacher's vision for the school. What was striking was how in most of the schools comparatively few teachers were able to speak with any confidence about the elements of the vision. This would suggest that, as a general rule, the headteachers of these schools had not consciously and deliberately set out to communicate their vision to colleagues and to ensure that its influence permeated every aspect of organisational life. Only in four of the schools were staff very clear as to what the headteacher stood for and wished to see happen. It was evident in each case that the head had taken steps to ensure that the vision was known about, shared and acted upon:
'Without pressuring, the headteacher makes sure she gets what she wants. She's always talking about it, making plans, discussing things', a teacher in one of the schools reported. In a second, a member of staff remarked on the continuous review and evaluation of the school's ethos and processes: *'The school is effective particularly because it questions itself all the time.'* To this the headteacher added:

> 'We have taken on all changes and absorbed them into the vision. We have been able to keep on course and use these things without losing our sense of purpose'.

The headteacher of the third school noted that staff would be aware of the vision because:

> 'they know that I'm constantly seeking quality and also evaluation of quality. In other words, the work we produce is under scrutiny all the time by us. I think they are aware also that I place great emphasis on relationships and (on) the value of people as people...(They) are also aware of the areas of weakness we are determined to sort out because they have seen the appointments made (and) they've heard what I've said...'.

Staff confirmed that there could be no doubting what mattered to their headteacher.

> 'It's partly the things that the headteacher plugs on the internal tannoy, what he says at staff meetings and what he says to you personally, because the

whole ethos is bound up with the way he treats members of staff — you can always find the headteacher should you choose to.'

The headteacher's comment confirmed this:

> 'The dreaded tannoy...the best form of communication I've found in any school. What it enables me to do is put my tone on the school...I think the ritual of that and the message that I can get over, and the way I want to say it, is important for maintaining the ethos and philosophy of the school, because I can reach all the people in the school.'

However, it appeared that the majority of the teachers interviewed in the schools visited had had to deduce or infer what the vision might be (eg, by noting what aspects their headteacher would enthuse about, draw to their attention or possibly allocate resources to, or what from among their own practice won praise). This they were well able to do, for the most part, and reasonably accurately — which would seem to suggest that, whilst most headteachers were not actively and explicitly shaping the culture of their school, nevertheless they were acting subtly to ensure that certain elements of the vision were realised.

The team approach to leadership

We began this section by recording how every study of effective schools had confirmed the headteacher as a major factor in the degree of success achieved. Undoubtedly this has much to do with the degree of influence which headteachers are able to exert by virtue of their position. These days, however, it is increasingly rare for headteachers to manage alone. For one thing, the complexity of the task and the sheer volume of changes to be managed render it virtually impossible for one person to be able to handle school management. Also there is increasing recognition of the benefits for all parties to be derived from shared management.

It quickly became apparent that many of the headteachers in the sample of schools were operating in close conjunction with one or several colleagues. This was as true of primary schools as it was of secondary schools.

Table 6 shows the means and standard deviations for the eight items on the questionnaire which focused on aspects of the work of the senior management team (SMT). Once again, mean scores on all the items for the primary sector were quite high, higher than those for the secondary phase in all but one case. The standard deviation was also relatively large on most items, this suggesting some marked contrasts in perceptions between teachers. A difference between the phases which was highly statistically significant was recorded for six of the eight items, only on one of which — senior management taking the key policy decisions — did secondary teachers agree more strongly than their primary colleagues. Overall, primary teachers' perceptions would seem to suggest that in most of the schools senior managers were generally supportive of their colleagues, though less so in their work in the classroom, functioned reasonably effectively as a team, consulted before making major decisions, and generally ensured that staff were kept reasonably informed. There was however some slight indication that staff were not always clear about the roles and responsibilities of senior managers.

Table 6: Leadership and the (Senior) Management Team

The head and deputy/senior managers:	Primary Mean	S.D.	Secondary Mean	S.D.	Significance
Provide good and consistent support to the staff	4.10	0.94	3.61	1.01	**
Work well as a team	4.08	1.02	3.78	0.92	**
Promote the school image effectively in the community	4.02	0.87	3.98	0.90	*
Consult staff before reaching major decisions	4.01	0.95	3.35	1.09	**
Regularly brief teachers about day to day issues	4.01	1.00	3.76	1.16	*
Take the key policy decisions	3.92	1.02	4.12	0.74	**
Teachers are clear about the roles and responsibilities of SMT	3.86	1.01	3.56	1.09	**
Support teachers' work in the classroom	3.83	0.89	3.18	1.05	**

The mean scores on responses from secondary teachers, though lower than the primary responses, indicated agreement with the statements. The lowest score was on the item about support for teachers work in the classroom. A possible explanation may be that this task was delegated to the head of department or faculty. The significance of the SMT as the key policy making body at secondary level was strongly apparent, as might be expected. However, a good many teachers took issue with the statement that senior managers consulted extensively over major issues before finalising decisions. There was a notable difference between the phases in this regard. This finding is of particular interest bearing in mind the supposed basis for the sample, and suggests that management may be perceived as effective without necessarily having involved colleagues in whole school matters, in spite of the emphasis placed on this by the headteachers of some secondary schools in our sample. Of course it also may reflect the greater size and complexity of secondary schools compared to primaries — with the attendant difficulties this brings of keeping all staff informed and giving them a stake in shaping the future development of the organisation.

Primary Management Teams

The concept of the senior management team is normally associated with the secondary sector. Yet there was clear evidence of a 'management team' in five of the seven primary schools to which visits were made. In the remaining two schools no such team was readily identifiable, although in one the headteacher stressed that in effect the staff as a whole functioned as a close knit team. Where a distinct team was discernible, typically this comprised the headteacher, the deputy and those teachers with senior allowances, making a group of between four and six people in all. However, in several of the schools, particularly the smaller primary schools, membership of the management team was not entirely contingent on seniority. Year leaders and other postholders, even 'A' allowances, in some cases were part of the team. This group would usually meet on a regular basis, say, every two or three weeks, for an hour or so at the end of the school day, to discuss matters relating to school policy.

Irrespective of its precise composition, it was evident that the management team was seen to work fairly or very effectively in three of the six primary schools and in the special school, less so in the other schools. In those schools where the team was perceived to be effective, the positive features mentioned by teachers were that the team members appeared to work well together and without undue conflict, that the work of the team led to sound management and decision-making and helped keep the school on course, and that the overall style of management was consultative. Thus, for example, in the case referred to above of the small school, the headteacher's claim that the whole staff worked as a close unit and contributed to the quality of management was supported by other respondents, including the Chair of the school's governing body. *'...One of the best schools for teamwork. Never seen anyone isolated. Always across the board decisions.'* A second headteacher indicated that she valued the complementary skills that individual members brought to the team:

> '...the mixture of personalities is okay. One teacher and I are very much alike in our outlook — good disciplinarians, able to communicate. The deputy head is very good at paperwork. The other member of the team has a lot to offer and gets very involved in language work.'

In a third school, whose headteacher was a strong believer in firm leadership and in providing a clear structure, within which staff enjoyed considerable autonomy, again an open, consultative approach prevailed. Although this headteacher worked particularly closely with year leaders, strong emphasis was also attached to discussing policy matters in front of the staff as a whole.

In the three schools where the management team was perceived not to be working well, the main reasons for this appeared to be a breakdown in interpersonal relationships and poor communication. Thus, in one of the schools, the team formally comprised headteacher, deputy and three team leaders, but it was proving impossible for them to work together effectively as a group because of a deep and serious clash of personalities involving the headteacher and the deputy. (Indeed, there was some indication to suggest that the headteacher had deliberately enlarged the team, partly with a view to acquiring allies, but also in an attempt to reduce the deputy's influence on policy making). The two individuals gave sharply differing accounts of the reasons for their inability to work together, which appeared beyond resolution as long as they both remained in the school. Staff were well aware of this division, and some voiced concern about it.

In a second school where the management team was reported to be experiencing problems, much of the difficulty was attributed to a combination of lack of explicitness and poor communication coupled with interpersonal difficulties. Here, according to the headteacher, the team consisted of the headteacher, the deputy and two 'B' postholders. However, three 'A' postholders were under the impression that they, too, were members of this group, having been present on specific occasions in the past. They had anticipated being regularly involved but, in the event, had been excluded without any explanation, this having led to frustration and disenchantment. One consequence was that the group was regarded by some of the staff as a divisive force. One teacher referred to a wedge having been driven between the management team and the rest of the staff. *'It is divide and rule.'* A second confirmed this.

'The 'A' posts are confused about the SMT. The idea was that they should join us when necessary, but they haven't been invited as the discussions have not been relevant to them. They feel that it is a closed shop, a 'gang of four' — and the main professional grades feel completely left out.'

It was further noted that the deputy headteacher did not fulfil a particularly prominent managerial role, concentrating instead on teaching. *The deputy takes a backseat. We get on well but we don't make many decisions as a group*, a team member reported. This was not disputed by the deputy headteacher: *The SMT have the potential to work well, but sometimes we don't make decisions when we should...*.

In the third school, conflicts of personality appeared to be the main problem. Although the headteacher claimed that the five strong team worked well together, and that meetings were productive, a rather different story emerged from the staff, some of whom were team members.

'It's not a decision-making group and we don't discuss curriculum issues...I don't think we work well as a SMT — the personalities are not always compatible.'

The deputy headteacher confirmed this. *We are not getting at the real meat, the meetings are not moving us along. We are not very good as a team.* It was implied that there was not always harmony among team members.

One school stood out, in that there was no obvious management team and little by way of delegation. The headteacher appeared to devote limited time to management tasks as such but emphasised the role of lead teacher — and conceived of the managerial role in terms of shielding staff from external pressures and from policy making so that they could concentrate whole-heartedly on classroom work. *I am there to protect staff and they are there to teach.* Unusually among the teachers with whom we consulted, the majority of the staff in this school were content with this. Most were highly supportive of the headteacher, and any criticisms were quite minor. However, one who was more critical described the consequences of this practice:

'There is not really a SMT, and that is part of the problem. The headteacher and deputy don't have regular meetings; staff meetings are held only once in a blue moon if something urgent comes up.'

In fact, the deputy headteacher claimed that she and the headteacher deliberately avoided formal meetings, choosing instead to meet informally each morning.

A possible explanation for this state of affairs, which is consistent with a contingency perspective on leadership and effective schools, would be that the approach was appropriate for the context. This was a small school serving a middle class catchment, where the emphasis was firmly on pupil achievement; and where there was a long-established and very stable staff whose objectives closely matched those of the parents, who were able classroom practitioners (in the traditional sense), had no great aspirations to an enlarged or reconstituted role, and were content to be left alone to get on with the business of teaching.

Secondary management teams
In all four secondary schools, responsibility for formulating and deciding school policy was vested in teams of senior managers, which ranged in size from three

to five people, with each individual exercising responsibility for one or more areas of practice. Additionally, in at least two of the schools, there was an extended group of mainly senior staff whose remit was to shape policy in specific areas. Over and above these formal structures, in every case efforts were being made to build a sense of ownership of school policies by extending the circle of people who were involved in reviewing current practice and debating the nature and merits of new initiatives. This was particularly pronounced in one school where every effort was made to consult staff, and to afford them opportunities to question or challenge ideas or to put forward their own ideas for consideration.

Each senior management team appeared to be functioning reasonably or very effectively, and whilst staff voiced specific criticisms, overall, considerable satisfaction was expressed, although it was noted of one SMT that it sufficed only in relation to the school's context. *'In a tougher environment the present management structure wouldn't work.'* Members of SMTs were especially positive. *'There's a feeling of immense support within the group'*, a deputy headteacher in one of the schools remarked. *'I think we work effectively as a team...We complement each other...I don't think there are any holds barred between us'*, a deputy headteacher in a second team observed. There was confirmation of this from a middle manager. *'It has got a management that is striving for improvement rather than being complacent.'* In a third school a voice at the grassroots indicated satisfaction. *'They are very good at getting people to do what they want...Everyone seems to pull together.'* At the fourth school, although the formal structure had the SMT — the headteacher and three deputy headteachers — as the nerve-centre of the school, in practice the potential sphere of influence was much wider. The headteacher was widely recognised as being an endless source of ideas, as an enthusiastic communicator and *'networker'*, very adept at *'management by wandering about'*, motivating and energising colleagues. Someone who took pride in fashioning a school environment characterised by mutual respect and trust among fellow professionals, together with openness, communication and interaction between individuals and groups.

What were the more common criticisms that staff voiced about the manner in which their school was managed? In three of the four instances, whilst staff acknowledged that their views were canvassed on most whole school issues, invariably their response was invited to a specific proposal, and only when a good deal of groundwork had already been carried out. It was not an open playing field, to use a sporting metaphor. As a teacher in one of the schools put it:

> 'Of course you can have a say, but by the time it reaches us it is not whether we should do it but how we should do it'.

Moreover, not everyone we interviewed was convinced as to the actual importance attached by senior managers to taking account of staff views and opinion. The feeling that decisions had effectively already been reached and that consultation was something of a charade persisted in three of the schools. *'It's cosmetic'*, was the reaction of one teacher to the school's much-vaunted system of internal consultation. In another school a teacher spoke about the senior management meetings which, unusually, were open to anyone who wished to attend. *'You can input things there, but you still get the feeling that several someone's somewhere have decided that this is the way we're going...'*. Where then did the real influence lie?

'It's mainly the SMT who decide how we are going to do things and then it's passed on to us to implement it, albeit in a very nice way. It's not a democracy — in that we don't all make decisions in a corporate way. Someone makes a decision and we can discuss it...(but) if they have decided this is the way we go, then this is the way we go.'

Acknowledging that many of the decisions reached were acceptable, this teacher made it clear that the process was not. Whether teachers' perceptions were or were not accurate on this issue, this was what a good many teachers often felt about whole school decisions. Consultation of this type risks being wasteful of teacher time and energy and of devaluing consultation itself.

In a third school, several staff referred to the late notice that they would quite often be given, and a lack of the relevant details, together with pressure from management for a swift response. The combination of these factors was felt to reduce the value of consultation. *'How can you comment from a position of knowledge and understanding if you haven't all the facts at your disposal?'*, mused a middle manager.

The other general criticism voiced of senior management was of what was perceived to be their over-enthusiasm for taking on new initiatives without always having consolidated existing developments. Even allowing for the multiplicity of government-led changes it was felt that some headteachers and SMTs were over-disposed to innovate. As a teacher observed:

'Because they like to be at the forefront of everything they tend to dive into something and see how it goes — which is fine but it can be stressful if you are the member of staff it has been handed down to'.

Furthermore, there was an indication from staff in at least two of the schools that the go-ahead sometimes would be given before matters had fully been thought through. *'Perhaps some of their planning is a bit woolly'*, a teacher in one of the schools remarked. In the second school the feeling persisted:

'Their (senior managers) philosophy seems to be one of 'Try this and adapt it as we go'. If you'd thought about it more carefully in the first place...'

'Let's set off on this course of action and see if it works, and if it doesn't we can change it. In doing so you put staff through a lot of stress and pressure.'

Comment

Leadership and the headteacher

Strong purposive leadership has consistently been found to be associated with effective schools (Mortimore et al, 1988) and headteachers have been identified as the key leadership figures in typical schools (Nias et al, 1989). Our findings support these conclusions.

The majority of the headteachers of the twelve schools visited were regarded as good leaders by their staff. Indeed, across all 57 schools a generally favourable impression was conveyed — as one might expect given the manner in which the sample was recruited. Where headteachers had been in post some time, there was clear evidence in a number of instances of their having built a team of staff who were broadly in agreement with their vision — thus producing a 'critical mass' necessary to effect fundamental change in a school's culture. When appointing new staff they paid particular attention to ascertaining whether potential recruits would fit in with the existing staff — both as a whole and to the team/department that they would be joining. Some among the headteachers were seen to be active shapers of their vision for the school. In some instances this extended to using colleagues such as year or curriculum leaders to reinforce their values, beliefs and vision with the staff.

Headteachers encouraged trust and openness among staff by being direct and forthright in their own dealings with colleagues. They set high standards in behaving impartially and in maintaining confidences. All twelve headteachers could accurately be described as people-oriented, although some were more adept at this than others. Most were highly visible in school and accessible to staff. The majority respected their colleagues' professionalism and sought to downplay status differentials, emphasising equality of treatment. They conferred value on colleagues by praising and celebrating their successes or endeavours, and showed concern for their well-being, attending to staff confidence and morale, for example, by putting things into perspective or watching for signs of stress. Most of the headteachers struck a good balance of pressure and support, knowing when to make demands of staff and when to ease off in the constant push for improvement. A number, mainly primary heads, stood out for their practice of asking probing questions of colleagues which went to the heart of the teaching/learning process. More typically, headteachers also acted as buffers, protecting their staff from external pressures, and many sought to prepare colleagues for likely future initiatives.

Most of the headteachers, to a greater or lesser degree, acted to involve staff in whole school matters, giving them a stake in the further progress of the organisation by canvassing their views and opinions. Further, they strove to empower staff by delegating responsibility and according considerably autonomy. They sought to foster a co-operative and collegial climate within school, in particular, emphasising the complementarity of the differing aptitudes and talents of individual members of staff, and the mutual benefits of teamwork. Generally, they sought to get the best out of their staff by accentuating the positive, and playing to people's strengths. Several of the headteachers displayed a particular facility for identifying aptitudes and capabilities in members of their staff which they were able to capitalise on for the greater good. The headteachers varied in their readiness to face up to problems or disagreements and to work with colleagues to resolve them.

The school visits prompt one further observation. Having examined teachers' comments, the power of the traditional image of the headteacher, as someone strong, dynamic and in charge, comes across forcefully — in effect, is the stereotype against which teachers measure their own head, albeit possibly unconsciously. To be sure, an element of modification can be discerned: notably in relation to adopting a more democratic mode of operating, including consulting and delegating more widely - which teachers welcomed. Although teachers displayed little enthusiasm for the out and out autocrat and management by dictat, nevertheless they seemed to need the reassurance of being able to feel confident that their head could be entrusted to keep the vessel safely afloat. Thus, more often than not, the headteacher appeared still to remain the dominant figure, was accepted as such and, further more, expected to be so. For any head to be able to operate successfully in a way which runs counter to this image, it would seem that he or she will need to be a highly charismatic and exceptionally talented practitioner.

Vision and leadership

Most recent studies of school management stress the importance of a vision to guide the further development of the organisation. For example, Caldwell and Spinks (1992) defined a vision as '*a mental picture of a preferred future for the school*'. It may be thought of as a beacon of light that beckons, its function being to guide forward movement. Educationally, its significance is that research has found a consistent relationship between the presence of a vision and the effectiveness of the school.

In the present study, all twelve headteachers of the schools visited had a vision for their school. In many cases however these lacked specific detail, and tended simply to reflect the broad aims of British education, eg, to encourage every child to reach their full potential by means of high quality teaching, teamwork and support from parents. Few really could be said to be genuinely inspiring, as the concept would seem to imply: vision/visionary ... The visions appeared to derive from the headteachers' own beliefs, philosophy and previous experience in education, and there was little evidence that teachers had played a significant part in shaping them. Furthermore, it seemed fairly unusual for headteachers to discuss explicitly their notion of vision with staff, and therefore colleagues generally were obliged to infer what the vision was about. That most teachers were able to do this with a reasonable degree of accuracy — nowhere was there a marked discrepancy in viewpoint between the headteacher's statement and staff perceptions — may be due to a common, taken for granted, underlying set of educational aims and values. However, this generalisation masks the fact that there were individual members of staff in several of the schools who appeared largely ignorant of any vision.

Three, possibly four, of the twelve headteachers stood out as exceptions to the rule, in actively shaping the culture and practice of their schools. Two were headteachers of long-standing, having been in charge of their present schools for over seven and thirteen years respectively, and could be said to have transformed these schools over this period. It was evident that they had thought about and formulated an educational platform. The other two people were comparatively new to headship (four and under two years respectively), but nevertheless were in the throes of enacting far-reaching change.

In the light of the literature, the implications of the findings are that headteachers, in conjunction with their colleagues, need to think hard about the future direction and purpose of their school. To be truly effective the vision must go beyond value statements such as 'A school where every child achieves their full potential', actually to envision what the school would look like if this was achieved.

The team approach to management

Caldwell and Spinks, 1992, in defining the qualities of the self-managing school make the following observation:

'Leadership which empowers others is central to success ... especially in relation to decision-making.'

They advocate multiple leaders in accordance with specific tasks, while Leithwood, 1992, refers to the effectiveness of organisations which emphasise participative decision-making.

Turning now to our research, one of the most interesting findings of the study was that patterns of team or collegial management appeared to be emerging and, in some cases, to be well-established, in the primary schools in our sample. Indeed, none of our respondents thought that there was anything strange about discussing the role of a management team in the context of the primary school. Implicitly, it was widely agreed that the scale and diversity of the management tasks merited some form of collegial arrangement. This would seem to represent a significant shift from the position of, say, ten years ago. Traditionally, headteachers in primary schools have been seen to exercise somewhat autocratic leadership — leading one major research study conducted in the mid-1980s to conclude that primary heads should involve their deputies in decision-making and delegate meaningful management responsibilities to them to a much greater extent (Mortimore et al, 1988). A more recent study of the culture of primary schools (Nias et al, 1989) emphasised the importance of collegiality, though mainly with respect to staff relationships in the context of teaching rather than management. However, neither study made direct mention of the concept of the management team at primary school level.

In fact, in the present research, more by way of a team approach to management could be discerned across both phases, and would seem in part a reflection of the greater complexity of the task of school management in the wake of the Education Reform Act of 1988. The number of innovations that have had to be introduced in a short time period is so large that no one person could reasonably hope to manage their implementation. Moreover, the technical complexity of some of these innovations also has made it imperative that traditional managerial responsibilities and procedures be reconsidered. There was clear evidence of local management of schools (LMS) in particular having had direct consequences in terms of the headteacher's role, this in turn triggering further change to the managerial responsibilities of other staff. Headteachers increasingly have found themselves being propelled toward a role more akin to that of chief executive, exercising oversight of the work of managers — in effect, functioning as leaders of leaders — rather than being directly responsible for every aspect of management related to the various discrete areas. As well as needing to devote more time than in the past to the public presentation of their school, key developments in the role of the headteacher have included providing the vision to guide the further growth of the organisation, focusing on longer term strategic thinking and planning, and managing the extended team of managers.

The role of the deputy headteacher would appear to have been considerably enhanced, embracing both new areas of responsibility, greater overall responsibility and more autonomy. In particular, the headteacher's focus having become broader and longer term has led to the deputy headteacher assuming greater control of day-to-day matters within the school. This represents change of considerable magnitude in the primary sector in particular, where, historically, deputy headteachers all too often have remained under-extended in terms of managerial functioning.

It was, however, teamwork which most characterised the management function in the majority of the school in the sample, the degree to which effective management was apparent reflecting to a substantial extent the quality of the interactions among team members, together with the willingness of those concerned to seize the opportunities which the wider delegation of management responsibilities afforded. In the larger secondary schools, although responsibility for policy making invariably remained in the hands of the four or five strong SMT, it was increasingly common to find a wider group, not necessarily wholly comprised of senior staff, who had a critical function to serve in terms of policy shaping. Where there was mutual respect, trust and openness between staff, few complaints were to be heard, teamworking being appreciated by all concerned because it brought into play mutually supportive relationships. With a backward glance toward the isolation of the traditional headship, several headteachers expressly mentioned how much they appreciated the benefits deriving from collegial working.

The one perceived disadvantage was that, in a small number of secondary schools, a gulf was opening up between the main body of staff and senior managers. Where the latter were virtually full time managers, sometimes they were perceived to be losing touch with teaching, pupils and their colleagues, and with the day-to-day life and events of school. Where these senior staff were respected, both as individuals and as teachers, and seen to be effective in discharging their managerial function, teachers appeared prepared to accept that this was an unfortunate side-effect of the increased volume and importance of school management nowadays. However, in those situations where staff were not kept informed of managers' deliberations and actions, and where the whole implementation of management remained shrouded in mystique, considerable resentment was apparent — especially if the school 'ship' was perceived to be drifting.

Three broad conclusions from this section are:

i   **Many of the headteachers in the sample had leadership qualities which went beyond technical managerial competence.** In particular they had good skills in motivating, developing and empowering teachers.

ii **A clear vision for the school's future was important** to headteachers and staff but in only a few schools had teachers contributed to its formulation. Too often the vision remained at the level of generality. Headteachers and senior staff should try to develop a practical and shared vision for their schools.

iii **Team management was a characteristic feature** in the sample, including the primary schools. The leadership role of the headteacher remains crucial but deputy headteachers appear to be much more effectively used than hitherto.

All three of these broad conclusions have considerable implications for the selection and training of headteachers.

Part 4

Structure, decision-making and communication

Decision-making and communication are centrally important features of life in every school and the manner in which these tasks are conducted can have a profound impact upon the overall ethos and the quality of work produced. The size of the institution is obviously a key variable; communication must be more difficult to organise between seventy adults rather than seven, and between people working in a number of different buildings rather than one. Yet there are other factors that probably have a greater impact in the long run; for instance, how open the headteacher and senior managers are prepared to be, and the extent to which they genuinely want to involve staff in decision-making about school policy matters. On a practical level, the effectiveness of the communication structure is also influenced, for better or worse, by individuals' technical competences (eg, the ability to write an accurate minute or a clear policy paper) and by their interpersonal communication skills.

Several of the questionnaire items addressed these issues. Table 7 shows the mean scores and standard deviations for responses to questions about the decision-making processes.

Table 7: Teachers' and headteachers' perceptions of decision-making

In this school:	Primary Mean	S.D.	Secondary Mean	S.D.	Significance
Each teacher has easy access to school policy documents and staff handbooks	4.34	0.80	4.12	0.91	**
Staff meetings are used for discussion about major policy issues	4.16	0.93	3.19	1.25	**
Teachers are regularly briefed by the senior management team about day-to-day issues and news	4.01	1.00	3.76	1.16	*
Meetings are usually well chaired	3.98	0.99	3.61	0.98	**
Teachers generally feel well informed	3.91	1.01	3.20	1.07	**
Working parties or small groups are used to investigate particular issues and to make policy recommendations	3.91	1.05	4.14	0.74	**
Meetings are usually purposeful	3.89	1.00	3.31	1.12	**
Teachers feel that they have a share in major decision-making	3.81	1.02	2.76	1.02	**
Meetings are kept to a minimum	3.57	1.21	2.98	1.19	**

These scores indicate that the majority of teachers in the sample agreed, and on a few items strongly agreed, that these features reflected the decision-making process in their schools. Again, the responses from primary teachers were very significantly higher than those from secondary teachers with the exception of one item, 'Working parties or small groups are used to investigate particular issues and make policy recommendations', where the secondary mean was higher. The difference might be due to the greater size and complexity of the secondary school leading to more fragmentation of the decision-making process. The qualitative data from primary schools indicated that the whole staff meeting was frequently used for detailed discussion of policy matters, whereas this was rarely the case at secondary level. Indeed the questionnaire scores for this item reflect this. The mean score was particularly low from secondary teachers on two items, they did not agree that meetings were kept to a minimum or that teachers felt that they had a share in making major decisions. At first glance this might appear to be a contradictory message but, as the written comments and interview data revealed, it appeared to reflect a feeling on the part of staff in some schools that, even though consultation might take place, it was not genuine, and their views were not really being taken into account. This finding taken alongside the low secondary score on the item 'Teachers generally feel well informed', presents a rather gloomy and indeed serious picture of decision-making processes in secondary schools. However, there were large between school differences, which we were able to explore through the qualitative data.

Decision making in Primary schools

The pattern of decision-making and communication varied from school to school, but there were broad similarities in the approaches adopted in several of the primary schools. The decision-making structure was usually simpler than in secondary schools since there were fewer people in the organisation. Four broad strands were distinguishable:

- headteacher and deputy

- management team or group

- whole staff meeting

- team meeting.

It was usual for the headteacher and deputy headteacher to meet on a regular basis, both informally and formally. Such meetings would deal with school maintenance issues and possibly, but not necessarily, with policy matters. Whereas an infant teacher commented that in her school, policy matters were *'discussed first between the head and the deputy and then brought to a staff meeting'*, there were other instances where development and policy issues were, it seemed, discussed from the outset with a management group or the whole staff. Since many, probably the majority, of primary deputy headteachers carry a full class- teaching responsibility, the time available during the school day for strategic discussions with the headteacher is strictly limited.

As mentioned in Part 3, none of the staff interviewed thought there was anything strange in the notion of a management team in a primary school, and several schools had well-established teams which, typically, consisted of the headteacher, deputy headteacher and one or two allowance holders (eg, a 'B' post). However, there was no set pattern and there were examples of schools where the management team did not include all the B allowance holders. Primary schools invariably have few allowances to distribute given their smaller size (ie, they are flatter organisations), and increasingly every teacher in a primary school has responsibility for a school management task. This may allow the headteacher greater flexibility when assembling a management team. A comment by one teacher helps to illustrate this point:

'we only have one allowance post so structure doesn't allow for incentive achievements'.

Where a management team existed it normally formed the first layer in the decision-making process; ideas would be discussed in this forum before being taken to the full staff meeting.

The full staff meeting was the arena most commonly used for discussion of policy issues with the staff, and in four of the seven schools visited the teachers commented favourably on the meetings.

'Policy decisions are taken through open discussion, we talk it through as a group in staff meetings. I definitely feel that I have an opportunity to contribute to policy making.'

'The head's style is that decisions are usually done as a whole school thing ...'

'I feel that I am sufficiently consulted if the topic is relevant to me; if I disagree about something I can say so to the head.'

The fact that there was open discussion about policy did not prevent the headteacher from providing a lead, as these comments from teachers in a primary school illustrate:

'He's very democratic but he has the final say ...'

'You do get an influence, but if he's against it he'll do his best to persuade you round to his way ... somehow or other he convinces you as to what he wants.'

The fourth level of decision-making was the team or group, and there were many different types of these (eg, upper/middle/lower school, infant/junior, year teams, Key Stage curriculum teams). It appeared that team meetings were mainly used to discuss curriculum and pastoral issues rather than whole school policy, but problems could arise if channels of communication between these teams and the school management group were not clear. For example, in one school where teachers perceived there to be problems with the decision-making structure, one of the issues cited was that the infant staff made decisions without consulting others.

'It's drift again. There is no clear decision-making apparatus. The two staff rooms and two staffs create problems. The infant staff make decisions without consulting people eg, the language co-ordinator who is in the juniors.'

Many of the current policy issues in primary schools are concerned with the implementation of the National Curriculum and, in meetings to discuss aspects of the curriculum, it was common practice for the teacher with responsibility for a particular subject area to take a lead in discussion of that subject and to prepare a briefing paper or even a draft policy document for the rest of the staff. The final document might be written up by the individual teacher or the headteacher. In one of the schools visited a working party of two or three people would usually be set up to explore a proposed new development or to review an existing area of practice, either subject-related or cross-curricular. The outcome of such exercises was often a policy paper.

Comments from primary teachers in schools where the staff were less happy with the style of decision-making indicated that the process could be hampered for a number of different reasons. In one school where the head said that decisions were made jointly, comments from staff indicated that frequently they didn't feel that this was the case.

> 'Policy decisions are taken arbitrarily really; there is not enough discussion. The staff with responsibility for a curriculum area draw things up and then we are supposed to discuss it as a staff. Things don't always seem to come to a conclusion and the deputy has to tie up the loose ends.'

In a second school, the issue was more to do with the lack of a clear decision-making structure and divisions between the staff.

> 'Depends on the policy. Curriculum, discipline etc, are whole staff discussion, then working parties, back to whole staff meetings and then they are put on paper. It's a haphazard procedure, there is no structure and it is too long-winded.'

In a third school, the headteacher saw it as his responsibility to shield staff from administration so that they could concentrate on their work in the classroom. Comments from the staff indicated that they had little involvement in decision-making, although the majority appeared to be content with this arrangement, and their broad views about the school remained very positive.

> 'It tends to be the head and the deputy who make policy decisions — I can't think of the last policy issue — you only comment if it concerns you.'

> 'We only occasionally get together — there are not many staff meetings. We discuss things on INSET days. We have not discussed policy things eg, maths, language. I am quite happy really and don't want a greater say in things.'

The occasional teacher took issue with the style of decision-making.

> 'The head and the deputy decide and then tell us. I would like more opportunity to discuss things, we can't air our views.'

These comments nicely illustrate the fact that teachers do not all want the same degree of involvement in decision-making, some will be content to concentrate on their class teaching and allow someone else (eg, the headteacher) to deal with matters of school policy.

The question about whether consultation was genuine was raised in a number of schools. This was one comment:

> 'Often feel that although we are consulted on major policy issues, the decisions have already been made, so in practice we have little influence'.

However, a headteacher in a different school commented:

'Sometimes I feel that consultation exercises are misunderstood, ie, consultation does not necessarily mean accepting a strongly expressed view.'

This highlights the importance of headteachers making clear to their staff, in so far as this is possible, how particular decisions will finally be made and by whom.

Decision making in Secondary Schools

Given their much larger size, it is unsurprising that the qualitative data revealed much more complex decision-making structures in secondary schools. These varied from school to school but were usually multi-layered and might include:

- senior management team consisting of headteacher and deputy headteachers (three or four people)

- a wider senior management group, comprising headteacher, deputy headteachers, senior teachers and D or E allowance holders (eight or nine people)

- a middle management group (heads of faculty/department, pastoral heads of house/year)

- department or faculty meetings

- working parties on specific issues

- full staff meetings.

The marked between-school differences in responses about the decision-making processes appeared to be influenced less by the structure of committee and staff meetings than by staff opinions as to the genuineness of the consultation process. In one of the schools visited, where staff were very unhappy with the decision-making process, the main criticisms expressed were that not enough attempts were made to consult staff about their views; that staff were not provided with sufficient information to enable them to make an informed contribution to discussion; that even when their ideas were canvassed there was little evidence that senior managers took account of what was said; and that they did not receive feedback following consultation.

'Consultation exists in theory, but little regard seems to be taken of staff views. Discussions are often hurried, and then at a later meeting it is said, 'this was agreed at a previous meeting' when in fact no decision had been reached.'

'Communication is variable. We are often not told of things until they happen ...'

'Too many decisions taken by the senior management team without appearing to consult. Especially fail to consult individuals sufficiently, rely on formal meetings.'

Similar points were raised in a second school where criticisms were made of the decision-making process. The school had recently been restructured, and policy issues were discussed in a number of different groups and committees. Though according to the headteacher this had been intended to empower teachers and give them a greater say in decision-making, several staff indicated that they felt the senior management team were the real decision makers.

'I still feel it is very much directed from the top.'

'Major issues discussed at staff meetings. Feedback, next steps are not communicated though.'

Of course not all teachers want to be consulted, as one respondent noted:

'Decision-making is too often passed over to be discussed at a full staff meeting. Not all staff enjoy being consulted on everything. I personally favour management who make decisions and explain them if the decisions are questionable.'

One way of handling consultation is via a written memo or bulletin, but whereas this strategy is likely to save on meeting time, it does preclude open discussion and so is not always popular, particularly if overused.

'Communication tends to be paper based and therefore very impersonal and open to misinterpretation with attendant problems of misunderstanding'

In a few cases there was evidence that teachers were very critical of the decision-making strategies adopted by the senior management. These comments come from teachers in two different schools:

'Complete top down management, with little or no concern for negotiation or consultation. Most (senior managers) are unapproachable.'

'Staff are only consulted or informed when contentious issues are not on the agenda. Major decisions are sometimes presented as fait accompli.'

'Staff meetings are sometimes 'managed' so that controversial points have limited discussion ... On some matters staff are fearful of making critical comments in case it prejudices promotion'

Whereas it can be argued that seven or eight people (eg, a primary school staff or a departmental team) may be able to take collective decisions, it is hard to see that anything approaching this model could be adopted for whole school policies in secondary schools. However, staff in some schools clearly felt more positive and more involved in the decision-making process than in others. Factors that appeared to make a difference were:

- when they felt that their views were taken into account

- when they were clear about which groups and individuals were responsible for taking particular decisions

- if, having been consulted, they obtained feedback about the decision that was made

- if they felt there was some flexibility in the process.

This comment from a headteacher in a school where staff spoke favourably about their involvement in decision-making, indicates a degree of flexibility on the part of senior management and a good deal of discussion throughout the school.

> 'Policy decisions are made erratically, systems here are not written down. Lots of ideas do come from me but they come from a lot of different places. It's to do with listening and talking at all levels, and the process of school development planning which involves everyone ... We move towards things; I hope that decisions are made where they need to be made.'

Several people in this school commented on the micro-politics of the school, whereby the headteacher fed ideas to the staff as a whole through a group of inner supporters, who in turn spread them throughout the staff. Two members of staff felt that ultimately decisions rested with the headteacher and senior management team, but comments from other colleagues indicated that staff involvement was regarded as important and echoed the headteacher's view that decisions were made at different levels in the organisation.

> 'Decisions are made through discussion in different groups. It depends on the decision. It's made where it's appropriate to do so, working parties, heads of department meetings, within departments ...'

> 'No policy ever comes down as a fait accompli. There is never a 'This is it ...' or 'We have decided ...'.

Staff views about decision-making in this school were very positive, and they felt positive about the school as a whole. The headteacher said that serious differences of opinion did not arise and referred to the policy of appointing staff who would fit easily into the existing pattern of working as a major reason for this.

In a second school where staff viewed the decision-making process favourably, there were two aspects that appeared to make a difference. The first was that the decision-making structure was clear and individuals were given guidance as to whether they had an advisory or a policy making function:

> 'After a lot of consultation which starts at senior management level, we then take it to the school management group (middle managers) and to departmental groups; if necessary we take it to a staff meeting and then to the governors before it becomes school policy. We make the point that the school management group is not a policy making group but a policy shaping one. Final policy is made by the senior managers after consultation with the governors.'

The second aspect that teachers appeared to appreciate was that there was a degree of flexibility about policy making; individual staff had autonomy within a broad framework to make policy in their own areas of responsibility. Comments from staff indicated that policy was made in all sorts of ways, that it was made at the most appropriate level and that they could always speak to the headteacher about a particular issue if they wanted to:

'It varies according to who is doing it. All policies aren't made up by the head, they are made up and developed by the people using them. If I produce a policy on special needs, I will do it and then discuss it with my line manager, one of the deputy heads.'

'The head welcomes people to talk to him informally ...'

'We are trying to get policy coming up more from the ground roots by setting up working parties on particular issues that anyone can join.'

'When we find that we have a situation where there is a lot of difference of opinion, we open it up for an evening and anyone interested can come to the meeting and we have a general talk (eg, on gender issues)'.

Communication

The focus in the previous paragraphs has been on the style of decision-making. A related issue, which undoubtedly had some influence on whether or not staff felt well-informed about what was happening in the school, concerned the means that were used to communicate information to and between staff. Procedures identified in the school visits varied from the basic to the highly sophisticated. Traditionally, small primary schools have relied on more informal methods of communication but, as the pressure of innovation and the amount of paperwork has increased, a number have introduced more formal methods. The contrast is illustrated by the approach in two infant schools. In the first, where staff thought the system was pretty effective, the main method used was to send notes round the classrooms to the teachers:

'Communication is quite effective and has improved. Week ahead diary for staff goes round, circulars from the office are distributed to staff, we don't have pigeon holes, it works on a tick system (ie, teachers tick when they have read the note) and in a small staff a lot of the communication is informal.'

The weakness of this system was that it could break down if people were away for any reason.

'Communication does break down occasionally, but it's usually if a member of staff has been away and we are overloaded. We have our weekly book that goes round so that everyone knows what is happening; we try to send notices round as quickly as possible; if you talk to one teacher about an issue you tend to expect them to tell their partners, you may not talk to every teacher.'

In contrast, in the second school every teacher had a pigeon hole where messages were placed; the staff room had a white board where key messages for the day and the week were displayed; every teacher had been provided with a filing cabinet in their classroom and each member of staff had copies of all the school curriculum and policy documents. One of the teachers commented about the head:

'She likes to be thoroughly efficient, and everything is business-like and well-organised. She is good at keeping staff well-informed about everything.'

Comments from the primary schools also indicated that though informal methods might work well most of the time, there could be irritating breakdowns in communication. For instance, in a school which staff reported had a good informal system of communication, there was a tendency simply to place notices intended for staff on a table in the staff room. This led to things being lost on occasion. In a second school the headteacher sometimes forgot to tell staff about forthcoming events.

'Communication is generally not good. We need more regular meetings to discuss policy and subject areas as a way to improve the effectiveness of the school. I would like to know more about events in advance.'

'This is the weakness in this school, we don't always get the information.'

'On the whole good — there are a few breakdowns in communication, but only little things eg, the head forgot to tell staff that the photographer was coming in.'

Secondary schools frequently report that communication is difficult, and given the number of staff, the size of the buildings and the sheer volume of information to be disseminated, it is not hard to see how problems can arise. In one school where staff were critical of the communication system, there were no general briefing meetings for staff and several individuals commented that feedback to staff about what was happening was poor.

'Communication is variable. We are often not told of things until they happen ...'

The school apparently tried to use a cascade model of communication, relying on senior and middle managers to pass on messages but this was not always effective. Yet sending lots of memos around was not always the answer either, as a teacher in a different school noted:

'Too many meetings and bits of paper circulating can lead to important matters being lost sight of.'

In a third school, several staff commented that a new structure had made communication very complex.

'There are too many people to liaise with to be able to communicate and consult effectively.'

In schools where staff felt that communication patterns were good, (though no one ever said that they were perfect), noticeable factors were the generally open style of management, which seemed to encourage wide discussion, and the use of multiple means of communication.

In one of these schools, the headteacher and several of the senior staff identified communication as one of their strengths and the head said of herself:

'I network. I listen and talk to all sorts of people. I go into the staffroom and socialise with the staff ...'

Several schools reported holding regular briefing meetings for staff and some also produced a weekly newsletter. Agendas and minutes from key committees were displayed on the staff room notice board in some places. In the schools where communication appeared to work well, the reason did not appear to be a technical one (eg, use of electronic mail); rather, efficient use of traditional means, staff handbooks, notes and memos, briefings, newsletters etc, and an open style which meant that individuals knew how to obtain further information on particular issues if they required it. Furthermore, a balance was maintained between personal and paper communication. Clearly teachers disliked being informed solely by memo.

School structure and staff roles

Three items on the questionnaire focused on this issue, as indicated in Table 8:

Table 8: Teachers' and headteachers' views of school structure

In this school:	Primary Mean	S.D.	Secondary Mean	S.D.	Significance
The staff have clear job descriptions	3.94	1.07	3.53	1.08	**
Incentive allowances are awarded mainly for management responsibilities	3.37	1.11	3.76	0.99	**
The current incentive structure helps in the achievement of the school's aims and policy	3.46	1.02	3.15	0.95	**

The mean scores from both primary and secondary staff were not especially high, though they did indicate agreement with the statements. Since the introduction of national conditions of service for the teaching profession in 1987 (DES, 1987), the broad framework of a contract has existed for all teachers. However, the responses indicate that many teachers still feel that they do not have a clear job description. The scores from primary staff were higher than for secondary, which might indicate that their jobs are indeed more clearly negotiated internally or, that because a primary teacher typically has a responsibility for one class, the notion of job description is not especially problematic. Agreement with the statement that 'Incentive allowances are awarded mainly for management responsibilities', was higher from secondary respondents than from primary. Two factors might account for this. First allowances in primary schools are typically allocated to teachers who co-ordinate a specific curriculum area across the school and they may not interpret this as a management post. The second possibility is that, since there are comparatively few allowances available in primary schools, there are teachers exercising managerial responsibilities without any additional allowance. The higher score on this item from secondary staff is to be expected given what we know about the organisation of these large schools. The scores on the third item indicated that neither primary nor secondary staff agreed strongly with the statement that the incentive structure helped in the achievement of the school's aims and policies. It is difficult to know why they felt this way. One could hypothesise a number of different reasons: for example, the allowance structure may have been allocated in a way that did not reflect current aims and priorities; it could be a comment on the calibre of the staff currently holding the allowances; or a judgement about whether the current salary structure rewards teachers sufficiently for the work they undertake. However, the question of job descriptions and allowances did not appear to be a burning issue with either primary or secondary teachers and it was rarely commented upon in the open ended comments or at interview.

Five items on the questionnaire were intended for secondary respondents only, and these explored issues to do with the structure of secondary schools.

Table 9 : Secondary staff perceptions of school structure

In this school:	Secondary Mean	S.D.
Interdepartmental links are encouraged	3.77	0.93
The departmental/faculty structure helps in the achievement of the school's aims and policy	3.69	0.91
The house/year/upper and lower schools structure helps in the achievement of the school's aims and policy	3.69	0.96
The pastoral and academic aspects of the curriculum are well integrated	3.34	1.13
Pastoral and academic roles are well integrated	3.41	1.11

The mean scores for responses to these items from staff in the twenty four secondary schools, though not especially high, were all above three, which indicates broad agreement with the statements. The lowest scores were on the two items that related to the integration of pastoral and academic aspects of the curriculum and staff roles. However, there were some noticeable between-school differences in the scores (eg, on the item about whether the pastoral and academic curriculum were well integrated). The lowest score was in a school where the responses indicated that staff had many criticisms of the school management, and schools which staff considered to be effectively managed tended to have high positive scores on this item, although there is no independent research evidence which can be drawn upon to aid interpretation of this. However, one hypothesis is that a school's provision for its students is improved when the pastoral and academic curriculum are integrated. In one of the schools where responses indicated that pastoral and academic staff roles were well integrated, a contributory factor would appear to be that the heads of upper and lower school had been made members of the senior management group and were responsible for co-ordinating the curriculum at Key Stages 3 and 4. Generally, these items were not ones that teachers chose to comment upon in any detail. However, teachers in one of the schools did hint at tensions that can arise:

'Too much time devoted to pastoral aspects at expense of departmental considerations.'

'An unfair system of allowances exists between departments eg, Head of Languages has a 'D' allowance, the Head of Art a 'B'.'

From another school two teachers made very similar comments about the way in which staff roles were allocated:

'Too many chieftains and not enough Indians'

'Too many administrators and insufficient staff teaching'

This remark by a third teacher provides the necessary context:

'SMT take decisions but they are not involved in practical teaching and hence the decisions are not always workable'.

Equal opportunities in school management

The issue of equal opportunities, though undoubtedly very important, was something that was only touched upon in this study. We have no data about the ethnic origin, age, disability or sexual orientation of the teachers in the sample but they can be identified by gender. Of the teacher respondents 60.7% were female and 39.3% were male; there were 19 women and 38 male headteachers in the sample, but of this number only four women were headteachers in secondary schools. This confirms what we already know from the research literature, that women are under-represented in senior management positions in proportion to their numbers in the teaching force. Three items in the questionnaire addressed the equal opportunities issue.

Table 10: Teachers' and headteachers' perceptions of equal opportunities in school management

In this school:	Primary Mean	S.D.	Secondary Mean	S.D.	Significance
Women deputy headteachers are not assigned traditional female responsibilities	3.70	1.00	3.59	1.12	**
The proportion of women in the staff is reflected in the number of managerial positions held by women	3.58	1.22	2.74	1.30	**
The proportion of teachers from ethnic minority groups in the staff is reflected in the number of managerial positions that they hold	3.00	1.07	2.96	1.26	**

The scores on these items are not especially encouraging to those committed to promoting equal opportunities. The highest scores were on the item about the roles of female deputy headteachers. Teachers in both sectors (again a higher primary score) agreed that they were not assigned traditional female responsibilities. However, this has to be seen alongside the responses to the next item about the extent to which women were represented in managerial roles in the numbers that one would expect. Though primary teachers generally agreed with this statement, secondary teachers were much less likely to agree with it. This finding is supported by these comments from secondary teachers in different schools.

'Only one female among a senior management team of eight!'

'No women are in post as principal or as one of the three vice principals, though there is a high proportion of women on the staff'

'I find it disgraceful that there isn't a single female head of year in the school — the impression this gives the pupils is that women have to defer to males!'

'Lack of women in decision-making/management roles and certain viewpoints may not be effectively taken into account or even expressed.'

The scores on the item about the proportion of teachers from ethnic minority groups who had managerial positions have to be treated with caution as a large number of teachers did not answer this question. The explanation for this seems to be that many schools did not have any teachers from ethnic minority groups on the staff. This important issue requires further, more specific study.

Comment

This section has covered a number of distinct but related issues which are central to the task of managing a school. Having clear aims and a vision for the school is one thing, but without an effective decision-making and communication structure the vision is unlikely to be translated into reality. The following points appear to come across consistently:

- **The importance of consistency between espoused values and practice**, or in other words the need for management to practice what they preach. For example, if a co-educational school has an equal opportunities policy for pupils and yet has no women in senior management roles then it is sending out messages about the role of women in society. Similarly, if the headteacher states that teachers are consulted about school policy issues but, in practice, the consultative processes are not perceived to be open and genuine, then teachers are likely to become frustrated and cynical.

- **The need for clear and widely understood consultative and decision-making procedures and for effective methods of communicating information.** Whereas the majority of teachers do want to be consulted about matters of school policy which affect their working lives, they do not necessarily want to be consulted about every aspect of daily school organisation and maintenance. A frequent complaint from secondary staff was that they were swamped with memos and meetings and that discussion of fairly trivial matters precluded discussion of major policy. This may or may not have been the intention of the senior management team. Owens (1970) proposed two generalisations that are applicable here:

  a. teachers do not want to be involved in every decision nor do they expect to be;

  b. an important task of the headteacher, therefore, is to distinguish between the decisions in which teachers should be involved and those which should be handled in other ways.

- **The value of an open, positive climate**. This is somewhat tautological as a good consultative and decision-making process is as likely to improve the school climate as be a consequence of it. Accepting that individuals differ in the amount of information that they like to receive or are able to handle, there would seem to be advantages in providing high quality basic information (especially about day-to-day management issues) for all staff; in establishing effective mechanisms for consulting staff about major school policy issues; in setting up enabling procedures so that those who would like more information or involvement know how they can obtain it (eg, publication of agendas and minutes, 'open meetings', ability to make opinions known directly to the headteacher or member of the senior management team without prejudice).

It seems that the decision-making process is less problematic in primary schools. We have suggested that one reason for this is the smaller size of primary schools. In addition it could be argued that there is a greater similarity in the role and job descriptions of primary teachers. The majority have a responsibility for a single class and teach their students a wide range of subjects, and this may make it easier for them than their secondary colleagues to develop a common sense of purpose and direction.

Part 5

Professional working relationships

The way in which staff relate to and work with each other helps to shape the culture and ethos of the school which in turn, it is reasonable to assume, has a major impact on the effectiveness of the school. The questionnaire survey had a number of items which explored the professional working relationships of teachers in the 57 schools. The tables below show the means and standard deviations of each of these items for the primary and secondary headteachers and teachers.

Table 11: Teachers and senior management

In this school:	Primary Mean	S.D.	Secondary Mean	S.D.	Significance
Staff feel their views are taken seriously by management	4.04	0.88	3.28	0.99	**
Staff are encouraged by the head to share experiences and success	4.00	0.91	3.31	1.11	**
Staff contributions are given recognition in staff meetings	3.97	0.94	3.50	1.17	**
Management tasks are delegated to staff at all levels	3.89	0.93	3.30	1.03	**
Teachers develop new skills by undertaking delegated management tasks	3.74	0.89	3.37	0.94	**

The first two items in Table 11 show that many primary teachers felt that their views were taken seriously by senior management and that headteachers encouraged them to share their experiences and successes. However, this was less clearly so in secondary schools, where the means for these items were lower. 'Recognition of staff contributions', with a mean of just below four, for the primary teachers indicates that they agreed they received this. Secondary staff were apparently less likely to receive recognition for contributions they had made to the school. However, the high standard deviation indicated that practice varied from school to school. The responses on the last two items in the table indicate that management tasks were more likely to be delegated to staff at all levels in primary than in secondary schools.

The most likely explanation for the primary/secondary differences, which were all highly significant, is once again, the greater size and more hierarchical structure of secondary schools. In a smaller school the headteacher and deputy headteacher can relate more directly to the staff and thus have a closer relationship than in a secondary school which may have anywhere between 40 to 100 teachers.

Table 12: Teacher-teacher relations

In this school, teachers:	Primary Mean	S.D.	Secondary Mean	S.D.	Significance
Go out of their way to make new colleagues feel welcome	4.43	0.68	4.06	0.92	**
Are encouraged by the head/senior staff to co-operate with colleagues	4.36	0.75	3.81	0.85	**
Are committed to working together as much as possible	4.24	0.80	3.65	0.93	**
Regularly discuss teaching methods/ approaches in some detail	4.12	0.88	3.31	1.08	**
Regularly engage in joint planning of new approaches to teaching/learning	4.08	0.97	3.41	1.07	**
Often seek and give each other practical advice about teaching	4.02	0.88	3.35	1.06	**
Experiencing difficulties receive support from colleagues	3.99	1.00	3.76	0.89	NS
Often prepare teaching materials together	3.93	1.01	3.40	1.08	**
Often observe each other teaching and give constructive feedback	2.59	1.03	2.32	0.98	*

The responses to the items in Table 12 present a very encouraging picture of professional working relationships between teachers. With the exception of the item on observation of teaching, primary staff agreed or strongly agreed that these features occurred in their schools. The scores from secondary respondents were similar. They agreed, though not to the same extent as their primary counterparts, that new colleagues were made to feel welcome, co-operation was encouraged and staff were committed to working together as much as possible. Discussion relating to the curriculum, joint planning and offering advice were perceived to be a feature of many of the primary schools, but seemed somewhat less likely to occur in the secondary schools.

It is interesting to note that teachers perceived that support was provided for teachers experiencing difficulties. The scores were somewhat similar in primary and secondary schools and the difference was not statistically significant.

The last two items in the table indicated that joint preparation of materials was not the norm for some secondary teachers in particular and classroom observation was relatively rare in most schools. Classroom observation is likely to increase once teacher appraisal begins to take place on a large scale.

The responses in Table 13 on school-wide relations are again very encouraging. Primary staff registered agreement or strong agreement with all the items and, with the exception of the last two items where scores were lower, secondary staff also agreed with them. The picture that is conveyed is of schools where a good team spirit was seen to exist, teachers saw their jobs as challenging, were constantly striving to improve teaching and learning and where there was a concern to build a learning environment for staff. Two of the items in this table strongly suggest that although many teachers saw the job as challenging, some were neither happy nor satisfied, and did not see the job as achievable. This probably reflects the stress and innovation overload which teachers experience as they try to implement the current wave of reforms. These are very important findings when one remembers the self-selected nature of our sample as 'well managed schools'. Teachers in other schools may well feel even greater concern about the current conditions in teaching.

Table 13: School-wide relations

In this school:	Primary Mean	S.D.	Secondary Mean	S.D.	Significance
There is a good team spirit among staff	4.36	0.78	3.83	0.92	**
Most staff see the job as challenging	4.28	0.71	3.98	0.79	**
There is a concern to build a learning environment for staff	4.28	0.79	3.67	1.03	**
Teachers are constantly striving to improve teaching and learning	4.27	0.64	3.88	0.80	**
Teachers are encouraged to be involved in seeking solutions to problems facing the school	4.25	0.75	3.67	0.88	**
Professional development occurs as an integral part of the job	4.10	0.78	3.58	1.06	**
Teachers feel able to express their views openly and honestly	4.03	0.99	3.59	1.05	**
Teachers feel happy and satisfied with their work	3.68	0.92	3.06	1.00	**
Most staff see their job as achievable	3.57	0.96	3.28	0.98	NS

Attempts to build a learning environment for staff and the integral nature of professional development, appear to be more evident in the primary sector. The extent to which teachers feel able to express themselves openly was examined in more detail in interview and appeared to be directly related to the climate created by the head and senior staff of a school. Professional working relations were also explored in each of the school visits. The remaining part of this section is mainly based on data from the interviews at the twelve schools, together with some of the open ended comments from the survey data.

Teacher autonomy

Most schools had established written curriculum policies or frameworks (based on the National Curriculum) within which teachers were expected to work. In the primary and special schools the framework was discussed at staff meetings and policy documents were then produced. In secondary schools, because of their size, more hierarchical arrangements still applied and policy was usually discussed by senior management and at departmental and faculty levels. Staff in one of the secondary schools had spent time discussing their vision of the future. As a result of this one of the teachers reported that there was considerable autonomy yet everyone had a sense of where the school was going. In all schools teachers had substantial freedom regarding how they taught but within an agreed framework.

Several of the headteachers talked about various forms of accountability. One primary headteacher examined teachers' fortnightly plans, having confidence in the staff to know that they would do well and that, should they have problems, the headteacher would be told. Headteachers stressed teachers' professionalism and trusted them to be self-managing. A primary headteacher who had adopted a very 'hands off' approach said:

'Teachers teach the way they want to, the class is theirs, the main thing is if the work is being done.'

A few headteachers made use of examination results and test scores as a means of monitoring standards. A secondary headteacher said teachers had considerable autonomy about how to do the job and that, with their heads of department, they decided on the syllabus, curriculum materials and teaching groups, but that they also knew that they were accountable for what they did. He believed it was the headteacher's job to stipulate outcomes within the aims and ethos of the school. This school had established a monitoring and support system in which each deputy headteacher had oversight of several departments. One of the deputy headteachers reported meeting seven heads of department every term to discuss progress. The senior management team (SMT) also selected a topic for the year, for example, 'Assessment' which then formed the focus of attention for the work between the deputy headteacher and each department. A system of in-house evaluation also operated where staff from one department visited another department and produced a report on their work.

Teamwork

Most of the primary schools had adopted a year team approach in which joint planning occurred at the beginning of the year with topic planning being discussed termly. Teachers shared ideas and resources and copied things for each other. At one of the schools the staffroom was used to mount children's work, providing an opportunity for teachers to see the kind of work being done in other classes. How well each team worked together clearly depended on the personalities of the teachers involved. As one teacher explained:

'It depends on the year group. Only two of our four teams work very collaboratively. Superficially it looks as if we plan topics together, but it is not followed through.'

In smaller schools with only one class per year, joint planning still took place among the teams of infant and junior teachers. In the schools where collegiality was most developed, staff talked about 'a team all pulling together', saw themselves as a close team with mutual respect and readiness to support colleagues, both professionally and personally. One of the primary heads said collegiality was taken into account when recruiting new staff and attempts were made to judge whether they would fit into the team.

While joint planning was the norm, team teaching was very rare indeed. In some of the primary schools teachers swapped classes occasionally, (eg, for information technology, music and dance etc,) but the full-time teaching commitment of most primary teachers made it difficult to work together in the same classroom.

One of the secondary schools had recently reorganized to produce house and curriculum block teams and this had begun to facilitate greater team work, although staff felt that extensive collaboration, especially across teams, was still a long way off. Staff at the other secondary schools confirmed that teachers engaged in joint planning and offered each other support within departments, but that cross-departmental work was rare. One example was given where teachers from various departments had jointly planned a study skills course. Two of the schools had suspended the timetable at the end of the summer term and some departments had linked together to enable students to work on a common project (eg, Energy). This experience seemed to have gone well and it was planned to repeat it at the end of the current year. However, the head of one of the schools noted that some staff were reluctant to work with colleagues from other departments.

Two of the secondary schools had used off-site staff conferences to plan and consider whole school issues, and saw these as very valuable ways of building a collaborative approach. In one of the schools about half the staff and four governors had worked in small groups on four main themes. The head, who was trying to encourage cross-curricular links, reported that for many teachers it had been their first opportunity to move beyond their department.

The other school had made extensive use of residential weekends, and every teacher had been on a least one in the last year. This school had developed very strong professional working relationships which extended into the teachers' social life. The majority of staff was in their twenties or early thirties and there was the sense of a very close knit community. As one of the teachers explained:

> 'A lot of work is done to bring people into the club, both socially and professionally ......To understand how this school works you have to understand the social fabric.'

Most of the teachers who were interviewed said they felt valued, and the majority believed that their expertise was being fully utilised. One example was given by a teacher in the secondary school mentioned above, who pointed out that the Chair of governors had been in on the morning of our visit to thank the staff for their hard work throughout the year. In other schools staff spoke of the importance of praise from the head and senior staff as a major factor in making them feel valued. One of the secondary schools had a system which linked every teacher to a member of the SMT, and staff felt that their particular strengths and weaknesses were thus well known. They saw this as an effective way of using their expertise and praised the headteacher and deputy headteachers for having the knack of slotting people into the right places.

(187) Information from the open ended sections of the questionnaire confirmed that teamwork beyond the departmental level, was difficult to establish in many of the secondary schools as the following quotations indicate.

> 'Professional working relationships in this school rarely cross the departmental barrier. Cross-curricular initiatives are rare, but this is not surprising when one considers the effort required to initiate them.' *(Teacher)*

> 'Within departments there is a lot of working together, but this does not extend sufficiently into cross departmental matters.' *(Headteacher)*

(188) These difficulties could stem from the size and complex organisation of the secondary schools. However, in two schools teachers reported divisions between the staff and the managers and low morale, which would pose barriers to teamwork.

> 'Very fragmented. Staff generally get on and help colleagues, but there is very much a 'them and us' situation between management and staff.'

'The staff are united by a spirit of despondency. There is low morale, poor working conditions, a heavy workload and a sense that the SMT don't care.'

A more positive response was given by a teacher in another school, who had taught at secondary schools in three LEAs.

'This school is the most advanced in joint planning and collaboration of any that I have experienced. It is remarkable how open the professional relationships are.'

A new teacher described the situation in a primary school where the headteacher had been in post for over 20 years and where new and old staff had very different perceptions of the school.

'This is a school in which good teaching takes place despite the lack of management skills at the top; perhaps because class teachers are aware of the need to compensate for these inadequacies by careful team planning and mutual support.'

A very clear message from the research was how hard staff were working to cope with multiple innovations, (this is discussed in Section 7). Several teachers in a primary school spoke of the pressure they felt under to try to keep up with their very energetic headteacher and deputy headteacher.

'All staff in our school work long hours on the school premises (usually 8-5 at least), apart from the work taken home. Both the head and deputy are workaholics (both doing a superb job for the school), but I feel we are under great pressure to follow their example. Most of us have families that we'd like to spend time with sometimes(!), and at present we feel guilty if we are out of the car park first.'

Staffroom talk and degree of openness

Teachers across all the schools visited confirmed that staffroom talk was normally a mixture of professional and social discussion. As one primary teacher said, '*A mixture of knitting patterns and children*'. The educational talk was usually about individual children and some curriculum issues, rather than policy matters. How open headteachers and teachers were varied across the twelve schools depending on the climate. Most of the teachers felt they could be open and honest and say what they wanted. A secondary teacher said:

'This is a very, very happy school and you feel you can make a mistake without being jumped on. There is a lot of support and if something goes wrong they will help you to sort it out.'

However there were differences between schools and the data indicated that some of the heads felt they could not be totally open with all staff. A primary headteacher said:

'I trust some people and not others, I talk about problems with other heads.'

In another school the deputy headteacher reported feeling wary on occasions and trying not to say anything personal, adding that it was the job of the deputy headteacher to maintain a positive atmosphere and lift the mood if people were moaning.

In one school where a rift had opened between the headteacher and some of the staff, one of the most critical teachers felt able to speak openly as the headteacher was leaving. This teacher reported that staff had been very guarded for fear of what would get back to the headteacher who did not take criticism easily. An attempt had been made by the headteacher to explore and resolve the difficulties using drama techniques, but this had not been successful.

'We are guarded, you have to watch what you say. We all know the head's failings and we worry what gets reported back. We said we would all support each other in staff meetings. There was an INSET day about three years ago, which was supposed to be a role play to let us talk about the problems in the school. It was a catastrophe. I think it was supposed to bring out the character of the staff but it was terrible, it all went wrong and there was no debriefing.'

Problems were also reported by teachers in another school who spoke of a split between the infant and junior staff. While each said they felt able to talk openly in their own part of the school, problems arose at full staff meetings where teachers felt very guarded and unable to speak openly. One of the teachers commented:

'I am very guarded. I think everyone is, especially in whole staff meetings. If I say things it might cause ripples. We were offered a confrontation session with an educational psychologist in the head's first term. I don't think we were ready but it's worse now. It's not to do with the head, it's just the personalities of the teachers. It was easier in the past. I am not sure if the head really knows about the problems'.

In a third primary school staff felt unable to speak openly in front of the deputy headteacher — *'you have to make the right noises and watch your back!'* was a typical comment.

The size and layout of the school obviously affected how teachers both worked and mixed informally. In one of the secondary schools, a new deputy headteacher made a special point of going around each of the areas of the staffroom where people were gathered mainly in departmental groups but perceived that the other members of the SMT did not do this. At another secondary school, senior managers were reported to come into the staffroom so rarely that when they did so en masse, staff assumed a major problem must have arisen! In another secondary school, a teacher said that he did not go into the main staffroom during breaks but spent his time in the sixth form block talking to other sixth form teachers. The special school had a particular problem which was mentioned by all those interviewed: each of the three buildings had its own staffroom and there was no common staffroom large enough to accommodate the total of 50 teaching and non-teaching staff. Everyone saw this as a serious barrier to whole school unity, yet the cost of providing a single staffroom was prohibitive.

Professional support and development

Professional development was given a high emphasis by all the headteachers in the schools visited. Two of the headteachers held annual interviews with each member of staff to discuss their professional development and career advancement, and this was welcomed by teachers.

One of the secondary schools apportioned their staff development budget between school/department/individual needs and, for example, had been able to pay half of the fees for a Masters course. They also ran their own in-house courses for middle and senior management and, based on the success of these, were currently planning a course for standard scale teachers. While the staff were normally complimentary about such provision, a teacher in another secondary school was critical of the reliance on in-house courses due to economic restraint and felt they could be 'very hit and miss'.

Staff in all the schools were asked what happened if a teacher was having difficulty. In every school staff reported that they would offer support. A teacher in one secondary school with a strong collegial culture said, 'We support and support and support. No one is left to flounder'.

The deputy headteacher in an infant school explained how a teacher experiencing problems would be helped:

> 'Teachers would have a little moan to me first and I would chat informally to the person concerned. The head would be made aware and we would talk about it, but would not become involved unless it became a major problem. I see it as my job to try to smooth things out on the shop floor.'

In the other primary schools the year leader and the subject specialist were seen as the first line of support. The headteacher would be kept informed but would only become directly involved if the matter was serious and then INSET would be offered. As a last resort an LEA inspector could be called in.

A similar pattern existed at secondary level. One of the headteachers who took a particularly strong line said that teachers were given plenty of support:

> 'but ultimately we will take action against them if there is no improvement . . ., we have had to do this with two teachers in the last 18 months'.

A teacher at this school confirmed what the head had said and gave further details of the approach.

> 'It starts with the Heads of Department offering support. The SMT on patrol are very supportive and regularly pop in and out of classrooms, they would have a discrete word with the person. Then the head would get involved and the LEA inspectors would be called in. If it goes on long-term then the teacher would be put on the line. Staff here welcome the fact that it is taken up, it's not threatening'.

School culture

Staff in the schools visited were asked about the various rituals and ceremonies which are to be found in all schools and are important in helping to bind staff together and develop the school culture.

A common practice in the schools was to bring in a cake for a teacher's birthday. In one of the infant schools staff and children sang 'Happy Birthday' in the hall and gave the teacher a birthday card. The headteacher in this school commented:

> 'They stuck a number 46 on my back without my knowing when it was my birthday. But they know I can take a joke. We all go out if someone is leaving and enjoy ourselves. It's much more than a staff, we are good friends. I have been teaching for 26 years and I don't know when I had such a good staff.'

Staff celebrations commonly occurred at the end of each term, with wine and a buffet and groups often went out for a meal at Christmas. In some schools staff would visit the pub on a Friday, and at one of the junior schools staff had developed a code of referring to the pub as 'the library'. If a teacher was unable to go to the pub she would ask colleagues to get her a book (sandwich) from the library. In another primary school staff said the deputy headteacher bought them little treats as, (a) a reward and (b) to cheer them up! In one of the secondary schools flowers were sent by the social committee if a teacher was sick.

In a further attempt to obtain information on the culture of the schools, we asked headteachers and teachers to think of metaphors for the school, the headteacher, the staff and the pupils. While some staff found this a difficult exercise, others used it to capture some of the complexities of their school in the form of powerful images.

These metaphors provide potentially fruitful insights into teachers' views about their school and the culture of the organisation.

> 'The school is like an elastic band, flexible. We do have to stick together and expand to accommodate new people.'
> *(Headteacher of Infant school)*

> 'It's the sea — constantly changing, fluid, but with real depth.'
> *(Teacher, Secondary school)*

> 'The school is like a calm, blue sea — usually warm and inviting, but with an occasional undercurrent.'
> *(Teacher, Special school)*

> 'Working here is like playing for Liverpool rather than Crewe Alexandra ... you're working hard and you're expecting to win things.'
> *(Deputy Headteacher, Primary school)*

In the primary school where there was a problem between the infant and junior staff one of the teachers wrote the following:

> 'The school is like a jungle. I thought long and hard about this, and although to call a school a jungle is a well-worn cliché, it is none the less true of this school. We are all fighting for survival in what has definitely become a very hostile environment.'

> 'The headteacher is like an ostrich. He runs from confrontation and buries his head in the sand — on the principle that if unpleasant and difficult situations arise, he can ignore them and they will go away. This creates

further problems in that someone else has to unravel the results, and someone else's decisiveness earns that person little respect.'

'The staff are like a group of monkeys and snakes. We have a group — the majority of staff, who work as a team chattering, encouraging, supporting, sheltering, fighting(!) together and for each other and most of all concerned about the welfare and education of the children — and three snakes who creep about and try to crush others, or use their venomous tongues to hurt anyone who gets in their way.'

'The pupils are like small creatures and insects. They need protecting and nurturing — but all too often they get 'trampled underfoot' by staff squabbles.'

'I feel very strongly that there are two distinct groups among the staff — those that put the welfare of the children first — and those that only have their own self interests at heart. The headteacher has not sorted out which is which — or chooses not to do so.'

Comment

This section has focused on the characteristics of professional working relationships between teachers in schools. The quality of the working relationships between non-teaching staff and between the teaching and non-teaching staff were not investigated though it is likely that these also have an impact on the general school climate. Traditionally, teachers have worked in isolation in their classrooms but in recent years the benefits of working in a more collaborative fashion have been increasingly recognised. After considerable research on teacher collaboration and collegiality in US schools, Little (1990) concluded:

> 'In large numbers of schools, and for long periods of time, teachers are colleagues in name only. They work out of sight and hearing of each other, plan and prepare their lessons and materials alone, and struggle on their own to solve most of their instructional, curricular and managerial problems.'

She went on to point out that against this backdrop of isolation, a small number of schools stand out. They are organized to permit 'reflection in action' and teachers work collaboratively. Little found that teachers in these collaborative schools:

- Talk about teaching often and in detail. Teaching is not the only topic of conversation, but it is a prominent one, and goes beyond the swapping of war stories

- Share planning and preparation. Colleagues jointly plan, prepare and evaluate their teaching methods and materials

- Frequently use classroom observation to provide systematic feedback. This involves more than just visibility, such as open plan classrooms, where teachers can see each other

- Train together and train each other. In these schools teachers continuously strive to improve teaching and learning and they share their craft knowledge.

Little summed up these four features as the 'norms of collegiality'. However, she stressed that in most schools what passes for collegiality does not add up to very much, eg, meetings on broad curricular outlines and school organization, but which do not engage in the close mutual examination of teachers' classroom practice. Schools with norms of collaboration are very rare. Barth (1990) agreed with Little's definition of collegiality and recognised that it is difficult to achieve. Nevertheless, he suggested that the issue of how to bring about a good measure of collegiality in schools belongs at the top of the school improvement agenda. He argued that unless teachers and heads talk to each other, observe each other, and help each other, very little will change in schools.

A study by Nias et al (1989) of primary schools showed that a collaborative culture existed in three of their five case study schools. The features of this culture were that routine help, support, trust and openness, operated almost imperceptibly on a moment by moment, day-by-day basis. Although this culture of collaboration was not formally organized, it was central to the teachers' daily work in these schools. It was found in kind words, jokes, gestures, birthday treats and little ceremonies, in the intermix of personal and professional lives, overt praise, recognition and gratitude, and the sharing and discussion of ideas and resources. However, discussion about educational theory, long term plans etc., was virtually absent from staffroom talk. Sharing was mainly confined to stories, tips and news, things which would not challenge the autonomy of the isolated classroom teacher. Leadership was especially important in building and sustaining the collaborative culture. This required leadership by example and modelling, and frequent praise for staff.

Hargreaves (1992) argued that only a few primary schools have developed a culture of collaboration. He suggested the term 'balkanization' to describe the culture of some schools. This is a culture made up of separate and sometimes competing groups, jockeying for position like loosely connected city states. Teachers in these cultures attach their loyalties and identities to a particular group of colleagues — usually those with whom they work frequently or spend time with socially. Balkanization may lead to poor communication, groups going their own separate ways, or squabbles and conflict over resources. As our own and other research shows, this is a familiar aspect of secondary schools because of their size and strong subject-based department structure. Obtaining agreement on whole school policies can be difficult in balkanized cultures. Hargreaves also suggested that a form of 'bounded collaboration' is occurring in some schools. Here collaboration is restricted in its depth, scope, frequency and perspective. The collaboration does not reach deep down to the fundamentals of classroom practice, but stays at the level of routine advice giving and sharing materials, it does not extend beyond discussion of particular units of work or subjects to question underlying values about the curriculum and teaching.

An underlying question explored in this section is the extent to which the schools in the sample were perceived by their staff to have a collaborative culture. Our data confirmed Hargreaves's notion that 'bounded collaboration' is the norm for most schools. The data showed that many of the behaviours that earlier researchers have cited occurred, most notably talk about teaching and shared planning and preparation, but there was little evidence of classroom observation and teachers learning together. The positive features that the data indicated were present in many of the schools were:

- **That the staff, made newcomers feel welcome, were encouraged to co-operate with one another, were committed to working with each other as much as possible and supported colleagues experiencing difficulties.** Primary staff especially, were likely to also engage in joint planning of work, to give each other practical advice and prepare teaching materials together.

- **There was good team spirit among the staff** who saw their job as challenging. The teachers were constantly striving to improve teaching and learning, were concerned to build a learning environment, and were encouraged to seek solutions to school problems. Primary teachers especially, agreed that professional development occurred as an integral part of the job.

- **Primary headteachers and senior managers facilitated good working relationships** by taking staff views seriously, encouraging staff to share their experiences and successes and giving recognition to their contributions. (Secondary staff were less likely to experience these forms of support.)

Part 6

Links with the local community school governors and the Local Education Authority

Clearly, schools do not exist in a vacuum. They are linked, formally and informally, to the social community or neighbourhood within which they are located, and for most schools also to the Local Education Authority (LEA). Historically, both have enjoyed representation on the governing bodies of maintained schools. No study of school management processes should ignore them. A further compelling reason is that recent government educational reform policy — as embodied in the 1986, 1988 and 1992 Education Acts — has direct implications for school management. For example, headteachers are now obliged to share with governing bodies responsibility for the local management of schools and the influence of the LEA is being severely reduced even to the point of schools being able to opt out of LEA control, all against a backcloth of enhanced parental choice. This project afforded an opportunity to study the extent to which the intentions behind such policies were beginning to shape practice.

Links with parents and the local community

The questionnaire survey contained a number of items designed to explore aspects of the relationship between home and school, and more broadly, with the wider community of which the school is an integral part. The outcomes are presented in Table 14. What is apparent from the data presented in this table is the prominence of parents as a key audience to whom school personnel must address themselves: hence, the time and energy invested in striving to build a positive and sound relationship between home and school, and to make parents feel welcome and at ease upon school premises. This goes further, in that across both phases there was every indication that teachers had recognised the importance of consulting parents on matters bearing on their children's education. In addition, although parents were apparently encouraged to raise questions about educational practice, primary teachers were much more likely to emphasise this than secondary practitioners. This may be indicative of the generally closer relations between home and school which tend to obtain at this age level.

There were indications that this investment of time and energy was paying dividends. For example, relations with the parents of pupils whom they taught were generally considered to be sound — as manifest in such indicators as levels of attendance at parents evenings, parents taking pride in their children attending these particular schools, and the degree of commitment of parent-teacher associations. Interestingly, a level of difference that was statistically significant was found between the phases on the latter two items, the secondary sector, unusually having higher mean scores, This may be indicative of the quality of the secondary schools in our sample, together with the fact that parents are more likely to exercise choice when considering secondary education for their children.

Table 14: Teachers' and headteachers' perceptions of school links with the local community

In this school:	Primary Mean	S.D.	Secondary Mean	S.D.	Significance
Staff work hard to build and maintain good relations with parents	4.48	0.65	4.36	0.64	NS
Parents are made to feel welcome	4.46	0.67	4.32	0.65	NS
Parents are informed and consulted about significant developments bearing on pupils	4.30	0.72	4.12	0.84	NS
Parents are encouraged to help in the classroom	4.28	0.90	2.26	0.98	**
Parents are encouraged to ask about educational practice	4.12	0.83	3.62	1.00	**
Our activities are responsive to the character and culture of the local community	3.81	0.79	3.71	0.85	*
Parent evenings are well attended	3.76	1.14	4.00	1.01	NS
Staff work hard to build and maintain close relationships with the wider community	3.70	0.91	3.66	0.92	NS
Most parents are proud that their children attend the school	3.68	0.93	3.94	0.84	*
There is an active and supportive parent-teacher association	3.54	1.39	3.77	1.14	**
There are good links with local community organisations	3.26	0.87	3.38	0.89	NS
Members of the community play an active role	3.23	0.87	2.93	0.88	**
There are good links with local industry/commerce	3.03	0.98	3.78	0.87	**
Staff play an active role in the community	2.80	0.96	2.83	0.88	NS

Notable differences between the phases are predictable: in the primary sector, the importance and prominence attached to parents helping out in the classroom, and the broad community orientation of the primary school; and in the secondary phase, the strength of the relationship with the local community — manifest in such behaviour as building links with local industry and commerce. However, across both phases teachers themselves did not appear to play a prominent role within the community. This may be a reflection of several factors, these including that not all teachers will live in the immediate vicinity, and the many within-school pressures to which teachers currently are subjected.

We turn next to examine what light may be shed on the matter of home/school links by interviews conducted with staff and representatives of governing bodies in the twelve schools which we visited. Broadly speaking, relations with parents were rated as positive or very positive in seven of the schools, and as leaving something to be desired, although in some instances improving, in the remaining five schools. Four of the five schools it should be noted, served communities with reportedly high levels of social and economic deprivation, where parents and other adults were perceived by teachers as reluctant to come forward.

In those schools that were in the majority, a cycle of positive reinforcement appeared to obtain. Invariably, these were schools which enjoyed a favourable standing in their community and the strong support of the majority of parents, and which were well-subscribed. All were schools where the staff worked hard to make parents feel welcome, informed and genuine partners.

In the schools where the links with parents were less extensive, teachers frequently bemoaned the lack of parental response, no matter how varied and creative their approach. 'Parents are apprehensive and wary of the school', one head wrote. A colleague noted that any trace of formality acted as a turn off for many parents. Elsewhere, there was reference to parents' own unhappy experience of schooling, to feelings of being intimidated, and to the hostility which schooling and teachers traditionally had engendered in those from working class backgrounds. It was further suggested that in the more socially deprived communities gossip and rumour often were rife, not always with justification. While it was acknowledged that schools in such areas were not all of quality, it was felt that the low image attached to schools sometimes was undeserved. *'This is seen as the sink school in ...'*, one headteacher declared, making it clear that he rejected this imputation. *'There is a lot of hearsay attached to this school'*. Staff echoed this. *'It's ill-informed gossip really'*, was a typical comment.

Interestingly, somewhat more objective evidence, which would appear to support the claims of teachers at this school, was to be found in a survey of attitudes which a member of staff had conducted among parents of the most recent intake of pupils. 65 parents, a high response rate, had replied, and among the qualities for which they praised the school were:

- the teachers were friendly and welcoming

- that teachers were thorough in communicating basic information

- the extensive extra-curricular facilities/resources

- that a premium was placed on equality of opportunity

- that considerable effort was expended in striving to involve parents in their children's education.

Less welcome findings from the survey, included those that teachers were perceived as:

- not always sufficiently rigorous in setting homework

- not enforcing discipline sufficiently

- failing to do enough to enable parents to become involved in their children's education.

Although based on a comparatively small sample, these are important findings which all teachers might usefully consider, for they give clues as to what parents are looking for from schools. While there will always be those who display a lack of concern and who fail to value education, there will be many more for whom the problem is more that of establishing a dialogue to which they can contribute and with which they feel comfortable.

In one primary school, staff had gone to considerable lengths to arouse parental interest in their children's education and, more broadly, to attract parents and other adults onto school premises — even turning scarce classroom space into a 'community room' with a range of facilities which inhabitants of the estate were free to use as and when they pleased. Nevertheless, there had been a limited take-up and mainly restricted to parents with children at the school. As for stimulating parental interest in their children's education, many of the staff expressed disappointment.

> 'It seems although we work very hard to involve parents we don't get much back in return', said one.

> 'Individual staff and parents make great efforts, but many parents appear to take little interest in their children', a colleague noted.

This point was expanded on by a third.

> 'Many parents see school as a place which keeps the kids off the streets and out of their realm of responsibility.'

Unfortunately we did not have the resources to interview parents in order to hear their side of the story. The headteacher estimated that there was a hard-core of around 25 parents *'who would be an asset to any school'* but that, as far as the rest were concerned their efforts were largely fruitless. Nevertheless they did not intend giving up their attempt to involve parents.

Governors and the school

The government legislation which paved the way for the devolution of financial management to schools also brought school governors significantly enhanced powers. In essence, governors are charged with governing and managing the school. One of the main intentions behind the legislation was to render headteachers more accountable for what went on in school. Headteachers are now required to account to their governing body for all aspects of professional practice. The survey featured several items designed to explore the practitioners' perceptions of the relations between schools and their governing bodies, and in particular, the degree of influence being exerted by governors upon school management.

The evidence reported in Table 15 suggests that up to now, only limited progress has been made toward increasing the influence of governors on school policy and practice. There was moderate agreement from teachers and heads to the first three statements below, although it should be noted that this generalisation masks certain important qualifications — notably, that a quite considerable number of teachers indicated that they did not have sufficient knowledge of the functioning of governors in their school to be able to make a valid judgement. Of itself this says a great deal about staff/governor relations. Across the phases there was every indication that, whilst staff and governors generally enjoyed a reasonably harmonious relationship, governors' influence upon policy and practice was perceived to be relatively limited. Governors were seen to defer to the headteacher as the lead professional on the majority of issues which came up for debate. However, between-phase differences that were highly statistically significant were recorded on the first three items, suggesting that somewhat stronger relations obtained between staff and governors in the primary schools in our sample and that, in the secondary schools, perhaps governors were being rather more assertive and exercising slightly more influence over policy and practice than their primary school counterparts.

Table 15: Teachers' and headteachers' perceptions of relations with school governors

In this school:	Primary Mean	S.D.	Secondary Mean	S.D.	Significance
The governors are ready to follow the head's advice on most issues	3.87	0.79	3.79	0.79	**
The staff and governors have a positive relationship	3.76	0.95	3.44	0.95	**
The governors play an important role in determining school policy	3.16	0.97	3.52	0.89	**
The governors' annual meeting for parents is a valuable influence on school policy	2.42	0.85	2.47	0.84	*

A specific strand of government action intended to enhance the accountability of schools to the parent, requiring that governors hold an annual open meeting to which all parents are invited, would appear to be failing according to our data. As can be seen from the fourth item in Table 15, teachers and headteachers were united in disputing the statement. Not only was this perceived as not having any real bearing on the evolution of school policy but, in many of the schools, teachers and even governors spoke heatedly of the considerable additional effort that went into preparing for this occasion, only for attendances to be embarrassingly low. It was widely perceived to serve little purpose, yet it took up precious time and energy which could be put to better use. The written report to parents was viewed rather more favourably.

What insights can be gleaned from the interviews we conducted of school personnel and representatives of governing bodies? There was strong confirmation of the findings reported above. There were only three instances where the evidence suggested a less than sound relationship between school and governing body, and in nine out of the twelve schools a reasonably positive and supportive relationship with governors was reported. However, this is not to say necessarily that there was extensive contact between governors and teachers. Indeed, in several schools the evidence was to the contrary. *'I wouldn't recognise a governor if I saw one'*, *'Governors and staff are very remote from one another'*, *'An august, remote body of people'*, were comments drawn from teachers in three different schools. Relations between headteachers and Chairs of governing bodies appeared stronger generally, as might be expected, although here again this was not universal. For example, at one primary school the headteacher and Chair were locked in a conflict of personalities. In a second primary it was felt that the Chair paid more attention to duties as a governor to other schools which served more affluent catchments. Even a fellow governor subscribed to this view. *'I think the Chair could be committed more — the name helps, but that's about all'*.

Asked about the nature and extent of the contribution governors made to school policy and practice, respondents repeatedly indicated that this was limited, albeit improving all the while in several instances. This was true of six of the twelve schools visited. There were only three schools where there was some indication to suggest a rather more substantial contribution by governors to management decision-making.

A sample of comments tell a clear story:

> 'The school would not change in any shape or form were governors not to exist.....(They) are still in the '60s.....still seeking a role to play.'
>
> *(Headteacher, Primary school)*

The deputy headteacher, who was a teacher governor, echoed this view:

> 'You've almost got amateurs in a professional role.....they're very supportive without interfering.....they're sympathetic.....they're very rarely critical.'

Significantly, the vice-chair did not dispute this diagnosis:

> 'We're here to oversee the management of the school but we're not the professionals, so we can't (cover) the educational side.....In a way it is a little bit frightening, because if you're not involved in the day-to-day running of the school.....it may seem as if we're sticking our noses in.'

In the event, they focused more upon 'bricks and mortar' issues such as the physical appearance and fabric of the school and financial considerations, rather than, for example, curriculum matters.

In a second primary school both teachers and the Chair of governors, though not the headteacher, expressed disappointment and dismay at the lack of involvement of the school's governors, 95% of whom the Chair estimated had not become involved.

> 'I am concerned about the effectiveness of the governors, and we need to invite governors, teachers and parents to work more closely together.'
>
> *(Chair of Governors)*

It was apparent in all of the schools visited that, to a greater or lesser degree, the stance of governors essentially was reactive rather than proactive, taking their lead from the headteacher and other education professionals, responding to information with which they were provided, or to issues which headteachers raised with them for discussion, and generally supporting and backing them howsoever they felt able. There were repeated references to governors being seen to rubber-stamp conclusions and decisions reached by headteachers and professional colleagues. Few indications were to be found in these particular schools of governing bodies actively pursuing their own agendas, although in a number of schools there were intimations that this might emerge in time.

Lest it be thought that we are reporting here the carping of members of the teaching profession, disgruntled at the greater level of accountability enjoined on them by the government led reforms, it needs to be stated explicitly that criticisms and reservations expressed in connection with the operations of governing bodies were as likely to derive from representatives of such bodies as from educational practitioners. Several Chairs of governors voiced their frustration at the limited impact which they perceived their fellow governors to have had upon the running of the school, and more often than not they attributed this to the same combination of factors: lack of sufficient knowledge of educational practices and processes; lack of time; and an absence of commitment. The latter generally was manifest in a failure to spend time in school outside of formal meetings of the governing body, although there were a number of instances where it was alleged that attendance at governors' meetings was poor. Furthermore, in a handful of cases it was reported that there had been considerable turnover of governors.

A lack of knowledge on the part of school governors was seen to be quite general, and although specific training for governors was felt to have gone some way toward countering this, the conclusions were unmistakeable: there was need of further training in management for governors, and possibly also for headteachers in order that they might work together co-operatively. Furthermore, commonsense suggests the need for a period of transition during which education professionals and school governors gradually build toward a joint partnership.

It should perhaps be underlined that for the schools visited, any concern at the formal authority which governors now command, in spite of their lack of detailed knowledge of educational practice, was more a potential than an actual concern. We did not come across any instances of serious disagreement between professional educators and school governors. Certainly in these particular schools, all parties appeared to be displaying considerable sensitivity, diplomacy and tact in an effort to avoid major confrontations. However, that there is the potential for serious disagreement is beyond dispute — a point to which we return later.

In so far as any general developments could be discerned in the light of the greater formal authority which governors now enjoy, this mainly took the form of seeking to extend their involvement in the life and activities of the school — most commonly by means of convening sub-committees to cover such areas as staffing/personnel, budgeting and administration, buildings/physical fabric, the National Curriculum and development planning, and by attaching governors to particular departments, houses or year groups. Such measures invariably had been taken partly with a view to extending governors' knowledge of the school, and increasing their capacity to identify with the school, thereby enhancing their commitment. It also afforded a means of enhancing their contact with teachers, where links were seen to be at their weakest. The headteacher of one secondary school remarked on the tendency in the past for well-meaning governors to go on a general walkabout around school. The headteacher considered this largely meaningless, in that it was not sufficiently focused, and expressed the hope that the new structure would lead to more purposeful interaction and involvement.

The evidence from the secondary schools where governors' sub-committees had been established, each being 'serviced' by a senior member of staff, was mixed. For example, in one school the Chair spoke of the *'harmonious but challenging'* relationship between governors and staff. *'The governing body isn't a tame poodle.'* However, in a second school the Chair indicated that, with the exception of the Finance sub-group, the returns to date had been disappointing. She was keen for governors to become involved earlier, at the working party stage.

There were a small number of cases where governor involvement appeared to be more substantial. They included:

- a primary school where the governing body met with the headteacher on a monthly basis, acting in the capacity of 'critical friend'

- a denominational secondary school where the strong commitment of many governors was frequently remarked on and the Chair told of how their deliberations had had an impact on school policy. Discussion on the length of the school day and of Key Stage 3 were cases in point. Even so, the view of teachers was that while governors were indeed quite active and well informed, in essence, *'they support the school in what it is doing rather than taking a lead'*, as a member of staff put it. Of particular note was the participation of governors in 'pupil pursuits' — tracking selected pupils through the school day as part of monitoring progress — and in the in-house scheme of evaluation, whereby staff from one department visited other departments in order to monitor the work of that department, including teaching and learning.

As reported earlier, among the sample schools all parties were able to co-exist for the most part quite amicably, and any tensions or disagreements tended to be minor and localised. The only real note of concern, raised by the headteachers of two of the schools, was at the increasing politicisation of the governing body. As a consequence, it was alleged that educational matters were not always being considered and decided on their merit. In one of the schools, where it was felt that the Chair had handled this very adroitly to date, the deputy headteacher observed:

'The governors are supportive but there is a political dimension. It was to the right and is now to the left.'

In the second school it appeared more of a problem, largely it seemed due to the influence which the Chair was perceived to wield over the governing body. The headteacher did not disguise the fact that she and the Chair did not always see eye to eye.

'It's very difficult to present an educational view to a group of people if a powerful Chair has a political stance.....If I criticise, it is not recognised on its merits.....it's seen as of the other persuasion.'

The Chair was accused of behaving in a patrician manner, for instance, co-opting a supporter with no connection whatsoever to the school onto the governing body, and of never passing up an opportunity to lambast teachers for the alleged shortcomings in the educational system. Especially galling to school staff was that the Chair and some among the governors spent very little time in the school.

'Some governors, usually parent governors, take an active and supportive role. The majority don't know the staff and do not seek involvement, even though they are encouraged to do so'

the headteacher declared. This prompted strong condemnation from the staff:

'If you want to be a governor you should take a more active interest'

said one. A colleague echoed this:

'I think they should know what goes on in the classroom'.

Here, as in several of the schools, it had led to a situation where the attitude among the professionals was to regard more favourably and to attach greater importance to the views of parents in general and parent governors in particular — even though their knowledge and understanding was not always extensive.

'I listen more closely to my parents than I do my governors'

one headteacher declared. A second headteacher spoke even more forcefully:

'The most valuable people to have on a governing body.....parents have the commitment, they're the people with the real vested interest in the life of the school'.

It was they who were the 'dynamic group' on the school's governing body — albeit 'the least informed'.

Relations with the Local Education Authority

Only one item on the questionnaire explicitly addressed this aspect.

Table 16: The LEA

In this school:	Primary Mean	S.D.	Secondary Mean	S.D.	Significance
There is a close and productive relationship with the LEA	3.26	0.86	3.10	0.90	NS

Findings indicate that, in many of the sample schools, relations with the LEA were not especially close or productive. This was born out by the interviews conducted in the schools visited. In eight of the twelve schools the strong impression conveyed was that, while relations with the LEA were generally sound, even good, there was little evidence of frequent and productive exchanges, particularly in relation to matters concerning school management. Of the remaining schools, in two instances relations appeared very limited, and in a third they were described as evolving. However, only in the cases of two schools did the relationship appear at all negative. Overall, the impression was that the sample schools enjoyed a satisfactory relationship with their LEA, especially as represented by the liaison or 'patch' adviser or inspector, and that should the need arise, support tailored to that need would be forthcoming. However, few LEAs appeared to have the resources to be able to operate proactively. They were obliged to ration and prioritise, concentrating attention on those schools where significant problems were being experienced. This was not the case for any of the schools that we visited. It is important to recognise that, far from voicing concern or dissatisfaction at this, the majority of headteachers and representatives of governing bodies accepted this state of affairs and were not unduly concerned, secure in the knowledge that they enjoyed the backing of their LEA and that, should it become necessary, they could call on it for guidance and assistance.

Only two instances of a more substantial contribution by the LEA to school management came to our attention — although it should be noted that in recent years LEAs in general have strongly encouraged and promoted management development in their programmes of in-service training. In the first case, the LEA had been particularly helpful when approached for guidance and assistance in relation to strengthening middle management. In the second, the LEA had strengthened considerably its monitoring of schools, by a variety of means, these including full inspections, departmental reviews and 'negotiated inspections', into which schools could opt. One of several purposes to which monitoring was put was to enhance management development. In addition, the LEA had a designated adviser whose remit included management issues in the secondary school.

Where the relationship was at its weakest, there appeared to be different reasons for this in the LEAs concerned. In one, it was portrayed as a straightforward matter of physical distance from the centre. *'We're the forgotten corner of (the shire).....the back of beyond'*, the headteacher declared. (In fact, the relationship with their 'patch' inspector appeared extremely sound.) However, a member of staff suggested that the school might well appear *'a thorn in their (LEA) side'*, in having responded so positively and capably to the need to develop a substantial level of self-sufficiency. With regard to the issue of management, the headteacher referred to the necessity to be self-managing and self-sustaining, *'because there ain't no cavalry out there.....It's no use my waiting for someone to tell me how to do it.....to hold my hand'*. Although the school had little option other than to go it alone, it should be noted that this suited the headteacher, who took pride in asserting its independence and individuality.

In the second case, the teachers perceived links with the LEA to be less than healthy. The headteacher, while acknowledging that they had enjoyed positive relations with three different 'link' inspectors in recent years, and affirming the capabilities of the present chief inspector, maintained that the quality of the services offered by the LEA had suffered due to staff shortages, exacerbated by the failure to replace very able staff who had moved elsewhere. However, doubt was also cast on the calibre of some LEA personnel.

> 'We have had some very ineffective officers who may not have the best interests of the children or schools at heart.'

This was a theme which others took up. For example, two of the teachers referred to the paucity of resources for schools, together with a general lack of support, whilst the Chair of the school's governing body, an accountant, was particularly scathing. LEA/governor relations were described as:

> 'at an all-time low because of poor resourcing and their lack of care about the children. There has been poor management and lots of incompetence .....There has been poor support for schools and the LEA has been diabolical on finances.....'

In the wider sample, one further instance of perceived shortcomings at LEA level came to our attention. This involved a newly established LEA which it seemed had yet to overcome initial teething problems. Various weaknesses were alleged, including inadequate leadership, lack of organisation, failure to recognise the demanding circumstances under which schools were having to operate, lack of realism, and the failure to build toward a constructive working relationship with schools.

Comment

Parents

Following on the Education Reform Act of 1988, schools have been obliged to be more accountable to parents than has been the case historically — something which most teachers appeared to accept was a positive development, even though they were not always convinced that parents set much store by this. However, there was little evidence of increased parental influence, particularly in relation to matters concerning school management. The general feeling among representatives of the teaching profession was that, except perhaps for those with professional backgrounds, the majority of parents were more than willing to leave the shaping of education to those who they saw as most knowledgeable — namely, the teachers. Nor were most parents, other than perhaps those who put themselves forward for the position of parent governor, perceived to want an enhanced role, which conceivably might incorporate an element of responsibility for school management.

In schools where the relationship with parents was reported to be strong, this seemed to be a consequence of the staff working hard to make parents feel welcome, consulting them about matters affecting the students and encouraging them to ask questions about educational practice. Responses from staff working in schools located in areas of economic and social deprivation, indicated that they found it harder to gain the interest and support of the parents. Alternative strategies for involving parents whose own school experience has left them disinclined to take an active interest in the school their children attend may need to be considered and trialled.

School governors

We noted in passing the considerable extension to governors' formal powers following on recent government legislation. On the whole we detected little resentment from headteachers and teachers over the principle of sharing control, though we would record that teachers sometimes revealed their irritation at what they saw as governors' failure to get into school and find out what was happening and to begin to build relationships. In part, this absence of resentment may be a reflection of the fact that, on the whole and in most of the schools, governors were still functioning largely in the time-honoured way, content to take their lead from the professionals and not actively seeking to shape policy or take decisions. Were this to change, as it could well do once governor awareness has been raised and confidence built, through a combination of governor training allied to the passage of time, choppy waters might well lie ahead. Certainly, there are some disturbing portents, vis: the recent case of Stratford School in Newham, which had opted out of LEA control, and the NAHT survey which disclosed a significant increase in the number of headteachers being suspended after falling out with their governing bodies (reported in The Guardian 25/5/1992). Arguably, little comfort may be derived from the sheer strangeness of the Stratford case (in which the headteacher eventually was fully exonerated), or that in the latter, the absolute total of suspensions remains extremely small. Were governing bodies increasingly to flex their muscles, then unless the sensitivity and mutual respect displayed by headteachers and governors across our sample of schools continue to be observed, disagreements could become quite common.

Our research has shown clearly that to date, more often than not, governors are very much the junior partners in school management. This appeared especially so within the primary schools in our sample. To be fair to governors, however, this finding needs to be put in context. It must be borne in mind that these are early days yet, and relationships between governors, headteachers and indeed parents are still very much at the formative stage. Furthermore, governors are having to contend with substantial handicaps. These include: that generally they are lay people, and therefore lacking the detailed knowledge and understanding of school and educational processes; that governor training is in its infancy; that often they have other, perhaps more substantial commitments; and the absence of established patterns of working to guide them. Given this, it would seem fair to conclude that for the most part they are doing a reasonable job under difficult circumstances. Indeed, it might be observed that the wonder is that they are faring as well as they appear to be!

None the less, the findings of a survey of governor resignations conducted in 1991 in seven Northern areas, a mixture of urban and rural, makes for sober reading. 29% of the 569 governors who resigned attributed this to lack of time. Over 25% expressed concern at being required to exercise control over financial matters, whilst almost 16% referred to the high level of responsibility overall.

What light does our study shed? The main implication which we would wish to underline is that if governors are to be better able to exert real influence upon school policy and practices, more than the combination of legislation coupled with rhetoric will be required. There needs to be a fuller recognition of governors' need for, and indeed right to, training of quality, together with an acceptance that an active partnership cannot be forged overnight. While good quality training is central, direct experience is also crucial. In this regard headteachers have a key responsibility to assist the process. For instance, there is a need to find means whereby governors might gain insight into the workings of the school, possibly by taking on some specific responsibility. Some useful strategies were noted earlier in this section: for example, attaching governors to particular areas of the school, setting up sub-committees with a remit to address particular policy matters. Certainly there is an urgent need to forge a fuller relationship between governors and teachers, rather than governors' dealings being restricted largely to senior managers. In this respect, teachers perhaps need to think carefully about the nature of the potential contribution that governors might make.

Headteachers might also help through their own actions though. For instance, rather than reporting in detail the outcome of extensive in-house deliberations upon a particular topic or issue, they could perhaps look to involve governors at an earlier stage, possibly by sketching rough plans and inviting comment and contributions, by thinking aloud with governors or sharing a problem with them — even presenting groups of governors with a particular issue or task to worry out on their own. Strategies such as these represent means of enabling governors gradually to become more actively involved in helping to shape the way forward, rather than simply being invited to underwrite a carefully considered and presented, professionally-led case. They offer ways of building governors' confidence, such that they can feel able to face squarely up to the responsibilities formally accorded them. And they ought to help build stronger governor commitment.

- **It would appear that only limited progress is being made with attempts to increase the influence governors have on school policy and practice.** Furthermore, the annual governors' meeting for parents, which is intended to increase the school's accountability, does not appear to be achieving this purpose as the meetings are frequently very poorly attended.

- **There was no evidence of serious disagreement between school staff and governors** in the schools in this study, although in a few schools the potential for disagreement existed.

- **Training for governors, especially in issues to do with school management should enable them to become more actively involved in school policy discussions.** It might be mutually beneficial if headteachers were joint participants in the training.

- **It will take time to fully work out the practical implications of governors' enhanced role in schools.** Successful strategies that have been adopted in a number of schools to help them learn more about what happens include: giving governors a brief to investigate practice in particular areas of the school, involving them in school evaluation exercises and providing opportunities in sub-committees for them to work with staff reviewing aspects of school policy.

The Local Education Authority

The present uncertainty surrounding the future shape and role of LEAs makes it impossible to foresee what part they may have to play in relation to school management. That LEAs will be able to maintain existing services and functions at their present level is questionable, and it is a matter for conjecture as to what services schools might wish to buy in from them — let alone whether they will be able to afford to do so. However, the main point to underline from our study is that the majority of teachers and heads found security in the existence of the LEAs and implicitly viewed their possible demise with great concern.

- **The study indicated that the majority of schools in the sample enjoyed a satisfactory relationship with their LEA.** Headteachers and staff found security in knowing that they could call on the assistance of the LEA should the need arise.

- **Few authorities appeared to have the resources to act proactively, and one consequence of this was that attention was focused on schools which were experiencing some difficulty.** The increased focus on inspection had inevitably diminished the LEA support role.

Part 7
Managing change

This is a time of unprecedented change in education with schools and LEAs facing multiple, large scale innovations which have to be implemented in a short timescale. While this was not a detailed study of the change process, we were interested in how the schools in the sample had managed change, and this was explored in both the survey and the school visit interviews. At the time of the study, primary schools were more likely than secondary schools to be affected by the National Curriculum, due to its phased introduction, and this needs to be taken into account when considering primary/secondary differences. As one would expect, the national, external initiatives predominated, but factors such as the arrival of a new head, various attempts at restructuring and other internal changes also had an effect on the schools.

The first section uses the numeric data from the survey to provide an overview of staff reaction to change. The qualitative data is then used to illustrate teachers' and headteachers' perceptions about what had happened in their schools.

Survey data

A set of items in the questionnaire examined headteachers' and teachers' views on a number of recent initiatives, and the tables below show the means and standard deviations for primary and secondary staff.

Table 17: Managing change

In this school:	Primary Mean	S.D.	Secondary Mean	S.D.	Significance
The head ensures that money/resources are allocated to support innovations	4.29	0.65	3.79	0.87	**
Collaborative ways of working help staff to cope with stress	4.11	0.84	3.48	1.03	**
Collaborative decision-making on change takes more time but leads to better results	4.08	0.84	3.59	0.94	**
We are coping well with the introduction of the National Curriculum	4.06	0.81	3.50	0.98	**
The current reforms have lead to increased collaborative work among staff	4.05	0.84	3.74	0.89	*
Change has been successfully managed	3.97	0.79	3.66	0.94	**
We are very receptive to innovation and change	3.88	0.82	3.55	1.07	**
We are coping well with the introduction of national assessment	3.48	1.07	3.19	0.92	**

The first five items in Table 17 had mean scores of over four from the primary staff, suggesting that they felt they had coped well with the introduction of the National Curriculum and that headteachers had facilitated this through the allocation of financial and other resources. The reforms were generally seen to have increased collaboration, which helped to ease stress, and teachers tended to agree that collaborative decision-making, although more time-consuming, led to better results.

As usual, the means on these items for the secondary teachers were lower, and the differences between the phases for all items were statistically significant.

Most primary headteachers and teachers thought that change had been well-managed and that they were generally receptive to innovation. But the introduction of national assessment was seen as more problematic than the other initiatives. Secondary staff were less positive about change generally, whilst the mean of around 3 for assessment reflects the fact that SAT tests had not commenced at secondary level at the time of the survey.

Table 18: Current initiatives

The School is making effective use of the following initiatives:	Primary		Secondary		Significance
	Mean	S.D.	Mean	S.D.	
The National Curriculum	4.06	0.75	3.61	0.83	**
The five professional training days	4.05	0.88	3.30	1.16	**
School development plans	3.90	0.79	3.67	0.86	*
The devolved INSET budget	3.80	0.84	3.47	0.90	**
LMS	3.56	0.91	3.96	0.87	**
School management training	3.50	0.80	3.41	0.81	NS
National assessment	3.39	0.97	3.19	0.84	**
LEA inspections	3.39	0.86	3.24	0.85	NS
Governors' new powers and responsibilities	3.32	0.86	3.39	0.76	*
Open enrolment	3.27	0.91	3.52	0.99	**
Appraisal of teachers and headteachers	3.09	0.96	2.76	0.98	**

The data in Table 18 indicates that most teachers felt that their school was making effective use of the National Curriculum. Use of the professional training days was seen more positively by primary teachers compared with the secondary staff, although the large standard deviation suggests that this varied across secondary schools. Local Management of Schools (LMS) was one of the few items in the survey where the secondary mean was significantly higher than the primary, indicating that use of LMS was perceived more positively in the secondary sector. This may be because secondary schools have had devolved budgets longer than most primaries and have larger amounts of money.

National assessment was again one of the lowest scoring items, as were LEA inspections and the governors' new powers. Open enrolment was much more likely to have had an effect on secondary schools, and received a higher mean score from them. Appraisal of headteachers and teachers had not really begun for staff in most of the sample schools, and this seems likely to account for the low scores. The primary/secondary differences were statistically significant on all items, except 'school management training' and 'LEA inspections'.

Interview and open-ended data

The following sections are based on the school visit interviews and the open-ended sections of the questionnaire. The main focus is on the National Curriculum and other current external initiatives, but some internal changes are also examined. Perceptions from the primary schools about the management of change are given first, and these are followed by the views of secondary staff.

The main positive and negative features are highlighted in the concluding paragraphs.

Primary schools

Most of the staff interviewed in the primary schools thought that change had been managed well. One factor which had facilitated this was the use of training days to brainstorm and share ideas. The effective use of resources was also seen as an important means of assisting change. In one school a teacher saw the improvements in reading and writing as the most significant recent change, and attributed this to the influence of the headteacher, who had allocated sizeable resources. Another teacher in the same school observed:

> 'Assessment and the National Curriculum are profound changes. The National Curriculum is good in parts as it has made us focus more thoroughly on our aims, and together with assessment, this has helped unite the staff in adversity.'

However, the Chair of governors at this school felt that the National Curriculum had not made much difference, in that 'it was all going on anyway.'

The flood of innovations had increased the stress on staff and headteachers had to try to help them cope with the pressure. The headteacher of one school commented:

> 'We are doing the best we can. I need to reassure staff that much of what is in the National Curriculum they are already doing. It's constant change that we have to come to terms with. At the end of the day I have to say to staff, 'enough is enough, go home'. The National Curriculum isn't the be-all and end-all, there are important things like having stable and contented children, because unless you have that you won't have any learning. We have to manage change gradually and realise that it can't be done overnight.'

Structures such as year teams and collaborative ways of working were employed both as a means of sharing the load and providing mutual staff support. One of the primary schools which had a well-developed collaborative approach had established year teams about 3–4 years ago. The teachers at this school saw this as a significant factor which had given substantial control of the curriculum to the staff. The headteacher thought that the National Curriculum, LMS and other changes had not been particularly difficult to implement because the structures were already in place and they were able to make the necessary accommodations without too much fuss. This headteacher saw the developments as reasonably useful, particularly LMS, but was highly critical of the low level of resourcing from central government. The headteacher believed that this could ultimately have a detrimental effect on quality, and was very concerned that the blame might be laid on headteachers and teachers:

> 'There have to be effective levels of resourcing, because if there aren't you get a cheap and shoddy product ..... If you want Marks and Spencer quality out of me don't give me Sunday market trading! There ought to be a minimum level of resourcing at the head's disposal in order to deliver the National Curriculum.'

Change was seen to have been well-managed by all the staff at this school. Many of the teachers mentioned shared decision-making and co-operative, whole school planning as the features which had influenced their ability to cope with change. The school development plan provided an agreed structure and set goals. The National Curriculum was seen as a chance to review and adjust practice, although the fast pace of change had still led to stress and feelings of inadequacy by staff.

Teachers were less confident that change had been managed well in a primary school where many staff indicated that they were not able openly to express their views because of the headteacher's inability to take criticism. They perceived that too many things had been left unfinished:

'A lot has been left up in the air, we need to finish something and put the last nail in. There have been lots of changes from the DFE and we have been wading in a sea of jelly. We need to have been more positive.'

Other teachers at this school said:

'Everyone is feeling harassed and overwhelmed and worried about assessment especiall..'

'No one seems to have much idea of what is going on.'

The headteacher had been appointed at the time of the Education Reform Act and was seen as responsible for implementing the 1265 hours working agreement. However, the headteacher had utilised the external pressure for change to introduce other changes.

'Some of it was unfortunate, but I was also able to introduce the changes I wanted to make. I admire the staff, they have had to take on an awful lot.'

Mixed views were expressed in a primary school with a new headteacher who had taken a 'softly, softly', approach in the first year. The Chair of governors was impressed with the headteacher's ability to obtain more resources.

'Lots of things are coming in now, it seems as if a barrel full of money has opened. We didn't know how the previous head spent the money, the details were kept from us.'

Some of the teachers also compared the new headteacher favourably to the previous one:

'Change has been managed well in that there has been nothing obvious, it's been gradual. Under the old head nothing really changed. Now the whole staff agree on the changes.'

'The previous head did not manage change well. There were too many changes coming with the National Curriculum in his last years and he could not cope. Now we are slowly getting there.'

However other teachers were more critical about the management of change.

'Change has been very piecemeal and ad hoc. We have been extremely bogged down by trying to decipher and understand the jargonised documents. Too many tasks have been attempted at once and not carried through to the finish and therefore not well implemented. We need more structure and long-term planning.'

'We have a school development plan but it needs to be widened. Change has been very difficult to manage because people's roles and responsibilities are not clear.'

'What change? It's difficult to see any change in the last year since the new head arrived.'

The present headteacher saw the innovations as beneficial, but like most people felt there was far too much, too quickly, which meant there was not enough time to develop things in sufficient depth.

In one of the other primary schools the headteacher saw it as a major responsibility to buffer and protect the staff from external change:

'I have tried as much as possible to shelter the staff from the initiatives. I am a great believer in INSET as a strategy to assist the process of change. We did lots on the National Curriculum, both in and out of school. I encourage them to go on courses. If we can't get supply I will cover. Change needs consensus, a head can't dictate things to staff. If you do it will fail.'

Teachers at this school greatly appreciated what the headteacher had done, but it has to be said that this approach stood out from the collaborative decision-making processes adopted in most of the other schools.

'The head has taken the National Curriculum load, but he should delegate more for his own health, he tries to do everything himself.'

'Change has been well done, in that it has been gradual. The National Curriculum has helped with continuity. There have been no directives from the head, it has been left for us to sort out. The downside is that we need discussion and more planning.'

The staff however were very confident about their teaching and did not see the National Curriculum as a particularly difficult innovation — as their comments show.

'The National Curriculum was a painless birth for us.'

'The National Curriculum was not a big thing for us. We are all keen on the 3Rs so the children did well on the SATs.'

'We are not working differently now under the National Curriculum. But we are more aware of covering the subject area and have to plan against the Attainment Targets. I was happy that what we were doing was the right way to turn out numerate, literate and happy children.'

The open-ended sections of the questionnaire asked staff to comment on the impact of the initiatives on the management of the school, the features which had helped them to cope with the initiatives, and their opinions as to how well they thought change had been managed in their school. The responses from one of the primary schools provide a good summary of the key points.

- **The impact of the initiatives on the management of the school**

  'They have forced us to reassess and review and led to more detailed and structured plans for development.'

  'More whole school approaches.'

  'A more hierarchical management structure.'

  'More discussion and involvement.'

  'A huge amount of additional work and responsibility in curricular areas being held by staff.'

- **Ability to cope**

  'The management structure was already established.'

  'The structure of senior team, team leaders, post holders, working parties and in-built flexibility.'

  'A stable senior management team over three years.'

  'Good planning and consultation.'

  'Head's leadership and willingness to involve all staff.'

  'Team work and delegation. Working parties to share the workload.'

  'The school is open to change.'

- **How has change been managed?**

  All the staff at this school thought change had been well managed, though the headteacher pointed out that staff turnover had been a problem.

  'Change is more effective if time is given to discussion, consultation and review first.'

  'The National Curriculum and record keeping have been tackled successfully.'

  'The professional training days have been well organized and productive.'

  Overall, the views of staff in most of the primary schools about the management of change were remarkably positive, although there were some comments in the questionnaire which underlined some of the more negative aspects of change.

  'The staff are under more stress. We see less of our head who has to attend management meetings. We are able to cope with the changes because we work well as a team. In view of the time scale and amount of change, I think we have done well and that our head has held us together —but we have had high stress and workloads which I am not sure we can keep up with at such pressure.'

(Primary teacher)

'There is increased paperwork and pressure to attend to activities that are not particularly challenging or are irrelevant to our situation.'

(Primary Headteacher)

'The head has less of a teaching role. INSET days have been run on stress management. Overload — thank goodness we still have waste paper bins to put most of the material into!'

(Primary Headteacher)

'All the developments are presently seen in isolation, but when our School Development Plan is finalised their inter-relationship will hopefully lead to a prioritising exercise and a more positive management style.'

(Primary Headteacher)

Secondary schools

As the survey data indicated, staff views in the secondary schools tended to be rather more negative about the management of change, and this was confirmed in the interviews, although circumstances varied from school to school.

In one of the secondary schools there was strong agreement that change had been well-managed and no real sense that the amount and rate of change had been detrimental. Indeed, the school appeared to thrive on change and openly to embrace it. The staff liked the idea of the school being seen as a model for other schools in the area, and it was universally described as a very hectic, dynamic and challenging place to work. People spoke positively about continuous innovation, trialling, review and evaluation.

'There is a vibrancy about the school which catches you up in it: you move along and get swept up in it.'

This was captured in the various metaphors which staff used to describe the school:

'It's a toboggan.'

'A high speed train.'

'It's the bubbling on top of a volcano.'

'It is like the sea — constantly changing, fluid but with real depth.'

Other teachers at this school saw it as a complex organism, a plant or animal, capturing the sense of corporate identity and life. The analogy of the amoeba was used to convey the flexibility of structure and constant shape-changing which was seen to have contributed to the school's ability to cope with multiple change. Staff at the school all spoke highly of the headteacher's abilities to create a shared vision and a collaborative culture, which facilitated the management of change.

The Chair of governors at another secondary school believed that LMS was a very good innovation:

> 'We have done a lot with LMS that we could never do with the LEA by managing the elements of our budget, and the school has benefited from it. We have the advantage of a high finance man as bursar, he was the financial director for one of the prominent oil companies, who was looking for a spare time task, having retired early. He has brought us all his wisdom and we have benefited greatly.'

At one of the other secondary schools staff had mixed views and were more critical of how change had been managed. On the positive side the effects of the initiatives were described as follows:

> 'There is greater emphasis and awareness of the National Curriculum demands'

> 'The initiatives have generally been constructive and used as a lever for improvement.'

The headteacher and a number of teachers thought that the main features which had helped them to cope with the initiatives were the appointment of two key people to the senior management team, which was working well together, along with the general team approach.

However, other staff were more critical:

> 'Chaos — too much being introduced all at once and no time to implement it effectively.'

> 'The developments have created a number of new management posts which have taken staff away from the classroom.'

> 'Greater line management — less real discussion.'

> 'Less time and energy is given to educational issues.'

Several teachers echoed what many people in other schools felt, that the changes had been introduced too quickly and this had caused considerable stress. One teacher said:

> 'The changes have been poorly managed. Staff on the whole are in agreement with most changes, but it has all been pushed through too quickly and often handled insensitively. This has led to a resistance to change.'

Another teacher raised a similar point:

> 'It puzzles me that management is over-optimistic. All change is presented as 'good'. If management presented some difficult initiatives more frankly, staff would perhaps be more co-operative.'

The following open-ended comments, which are drawn from staff in five schools, indicate some of the negative features which were seen to have resulted from the changes in many of the secondary schools in the survey:

'The initiatives have lowered morale, made teachers feel inadequate, put them under enormous pressure and increased their workload.'

(Secondary Headteacher)

'The school management team has been restructured but there is less time for teaching for those with management responsibility.'

(Secondary teacher)

'Management have become more remote and withdrawn from school life.'

(Secondary teacher)

'The secondary management team are square pegs in round holes with new titles.'

(Secondary teacher)

'The ostrich position is usually adopted on change. This leads to chaos and last minute fudging.'

(Secondary teacher)

'The senior management team are less approachable and available and hence it takes longer to get agreement. Crisis management.'

(Secondary teacher)

'There are more senior posts, more committees and meetings. Less contact with day-to-day classroom teaching. There is an enormous well of knowledge, skills, experience and goodwill among the staff, but we are generally discouraged and depressed. We feel we are being expected to jump through hoop after hoop.'

(Secondary teacher)

'At the receiving end, it feels as though management are struggling to cope with current changes and failing to inspire confidence among the 'deliverers'.

(Secondary teacher)

Management of change in a special school

This section provides a description of the management of change in a special school which had recently undertaken major restructuring in an attempt to alter its formal hierarchical structures. A new headteacher arrived about two years ago and felt that the school was 'begging for change'. The twenty four teachers and a similar number of classroom support staff work with 178 children and young people aged 2–19 in three buildings. The previous headteacher had looked after one building, a deputy ran another one, and a 'C' postholder managed the FE building.

The changes introduced by the new headteacher included a major restructuring, a whole school approach, increased INSET and the trialling of professional development portfolios and appraisal. The restructuring consisted of an enlarged senior management team (seven) with new people and new roles; all staff working in three curriculum groups (primary/secondary/FE); six administration teams and cross-curricular co-ordinators. The headteacher pointed out that the new structure gave a flattened hierarchy so that in addition to the school teacher management team, eleven of the twenty-four staff had leadership roles. Each of the groups and teams had a devolved budget and took on decision-making roles.

The new headteacher had wanted to break down the isolation of the three buildings and develop a whole school approach. The following quotations are taken from the interview with the headteacher:

'I talked to each of the staff about the new structure which I had in my head. People said that the small teams (building oriented) worked well, but there was no cross-site working and the whole school approach was missing. So there was no massive resistance to the new structure — a few of the senior staff left. We were also very lucky that there had been an increase in the school group size just before I came and this gave us more senior posts. After the interviews I presented a summary of the strengths and areas of weakness to the staff — the strengths far outweighed the weaknesses. All 50 people gave input to our three year plan and the senior management team went off-site to work on it. But they saw everything as a priority and put almost all of it in the first year of the plan. This forced us to prioritise more carefully. I had to remove a lot of guilt and say to them, Don't worry about it, we will do some things later eg, record keeping and resources.'

The headteacher felt that the restructuring had begun the process of staff empowerment:

'I believe that teachers and non-teachers are now in charge of their own situation. Two-thirds of the budget has left my hands and gone to the various teams. Everyone is a manager in the school — I preach that message incessantly. But if you get good devolved management, what should the senior management team do? They are not making many decisions now, so what should they do? We need to establish the climate and ethos of the school. Our role is strategic planning — to discuss and plan for the future and keep checking that we are on track. We have to pick up the initiatives and refine them. It's new to all of us, but it seems to be working, and more people are doing things for themselves. Decisions are made by teams and individuals at all levels.'

'I sent a questionnaire to all staff to get their views on the new structure and followed it up recently. They all showed a good understanding and it seems to be progressing well. We have an excellent staff. Of the fifty people here there are probably only three or four who want limited involvement, and no one is going against the tide.'

All the staff spoke about the considerable changes in the school since the new head's arrival. Their views can be seen from the following quotations taken from the interviews and questionnaires:

'The new senior management team is working well as a team. There is a good balance of personalities and experience. We are now comfortable enough to disagree with each other and it is very productive.'

'The new head has managed things very well. The expanded senior management team is very supportive to the head. The greatest barrier to further development is people's desire to hang on to the old ways eg, in recording and curriculum. But this is only a small number of people and they will be carried along.'

'With the previous head the National Curriculum was a headache and we plodded when it first came out — it took weeks to do the sub-targets. Then the new head arrived and we did it much more quickly, there was a different attitude. Some people still say 'Is it appropriate for our children?', but we are now able to see how to slot it into our needs. People are more involved now. I am very happy here and so are most staff — we want the changes to continue.'

'The previous head didn't give us much insight into the National Curriculum.'

'There has been an immense amount of change, the buildings, management, records, appraisal, curriculum, etc, every aspect of the school. It's surprising that people are not going around with frowns on their faces!'

'The new structure allows staff to have ownership of the policies. Staff are involved in all stages of planning the school aims and policies.'

'It is a good structure — everyone is involved in decision-making.'

'The head wants an inter-related web, rather than a hierarchical structure.'

'We are working much more as a whole unit now. The changes have been handled with excellent care and consideration for all staff.'

'Change is being managed very well. There will always be some resistance, people are at different stages and respond in different ways. We are sometimes put off by the few, but we need to say how can we help them through it and not just see them as the opposition.'

As can be seen from the staff comments, the changes and restructuring have been well received. This school provides an interesting example of 'transformational leadership' where the head is working to transfer the whole school culture. (Leithwood and Jantzi, 1990)

Comment

It is clear that all the schools were suffering from innovation overload, but some seemed to have coped better than others. The National Curriculum was seen positively to have provided a useful framework with which to review practice and ensure greater continuity. However, on the negative side there was considerable agreement that too much was demanded too quickly. The large number of initiatives and the short time scale had caused considerable stress and feelings of inadequacy for many staff. In some schools many initiatives had been left up in the air and had not been fully implemented. A number of teachers (mainly at secondary level) felt it had led to crisis management and a lack of overall direction in their schools. Primary heads were having to deal with considerably more administration and paperwork, which had reduced the amount of teaching they undertook. In a similar way some of the secondary school staff felt that senior management had been taken further away from classroom issues.

In the schools where staff felt more positive about the management of change, teachers talked about gradual change and having structures already in place. At primary level the structure usually consisted of year teams and other collaborative planning groups who engaged in a whole school approach and shared decision-making. The school development plan had provided the vehicle for some schools to prioritise the initiatives and produce action plans. Resources such as time, money and INSET had to be used to facilitate the management of change. Local Management of Schools was seen more positively in secondary schools. Headteachers and other senior staff needed to show concern and consideration for the effects of innovation on the staff and reassure teachers about their capabilities, skills and expertise.

Flexibility was an important factor in coping with the dynamic and rapidly changing situation. It is interesting to note that a similar turbulent state of affairs exists in business which has been captured by the titles 'Thriving on Chaos' — Peters (1988) and 'Riding the Waves of Change' — Morgan (1991). These authors argue that new management techniques have to be adopted in order to succeed in a dramatically changed world. Schools, like the successful companies who have had to develop new management approaches, need to use more strategic planning techniques as part of their school development plan. The other key factor is the need for a shared vision which acts as a beacon or compass to help the school with direction-finding in order to move forward using an incremental approach to change. This is well expressed by Fullan (1991) who says 'Think big, start small' eg, introduce change gradually, but within a clear long-term grand design.

In summary the main factors which appeared to help staff in these schools manage change well were the following:

- **The headteacher and senior staff made use of a clear communication and decision-making structure** to consult teachers about the nature and scope of the change in advance.

- **Attention was paid to how the change would be implemented** and the SMT tried to ensure that it was integrated with the whole school development plan rather than treating it as an isolated initiative. The SMT were sensitive to staff workloads and stress levels and phased in change at a pace that the organisation could cope with.

- **The SMT monitored how the change was being implemented** and adapted and modified their strategy as required.

- **Staff were encouraged to help each other to implement change** by working collaboratively where appropriate. The SMT ensured that they did not become remote from the classroom but kept in touch with staff views and concerns.

Part 8

Two examples of effective school management

This part contains examples of two schools, one primary and one secondary, each of which was perceived by the headteacher and a sample of the staff to be effectively managed. The two schools had high Z-scores on the five 'outcome' and ten 'process' questionnaire items that were used to select the twelve schools visited by the research team; they are identified as schools A and B on the quadrant diagrams in appendix 4. The examples are based on teacher and headteacher responses to the questionnaire and interviews.

The preceding chapters have presented a generalised account of effective management across 57 schools which is inevitably somewhat atomistic and de-contextualised. Our purpose in this chapter is to present holistic and contextualised accounts of specific schools to illustrate how effective management is a multi-faceted and inter-active process. The staff in these schools judged them to be well-managed, which is not to say that they thought there was no possible room for improvement. We have attempted to highlight the processes and behaviours which appeared to have led them to make this conclusion. The underlying question being addressed here is: 'What does a well-managed school look like as a whole?'

EXAMPLE A: WATERFIELDS SCHOOL (*a pseudonym*)

School context

This was a junior school, with 245 students on roll and a staff of 8 teachers plus the head (8.5 fte). The school was located in a small market town in a large shire county. The majority of students came from the immediate vicinity. The school catchment was described by the headteacher as somewhat above average, eg, the incidence of privately owned homes; the distribution of ability as average to above. The school also contained a number of students with recognised special needs, although these were mainly catered for separately, having their own specialist teacher and following individualised programmes of work.

The school was single storey. Most of the buildings were fairly old. Nevertheless, a combination of fresh paint, furniture and extensive displays of students' work gave a stimulating feeling. The overall atmosphere was one of warmth, friendliness, informality and hard work.

The school was organised on a year group basis (mixed ability), each year having a team of two (year leader and partner). The management structure comprised a management team of headteacher and the four year leaders, one of whom was the deputy headteacher. An aspect of the school's distinctiveness was that it was not hierarchical. Thus, the year leaders were the deputy headteacher, one teacher with a 'B' allowance, and two teachers with 'A' allowances. However, seven of the staff exercised a curriculum responsibility, the sole exception being a probationary teacher, and were accountable to the planning co-ordinator.

The school was headed by a strong individual with well-developed views, who had been in teaching for over 30 years. This was his third headship. He had been at the school as headteacher for 13 years.

Perceptions of effectiveness

The headteacher and staff were unanimous in perceiving that theirs was an effective school, both in terms of the education provided for the students and the professional development of the staff.

In respect of the *education* provided, quality was the key feature, as a consequence of:

- high teacher expectations of the students

- the genuine care and concern which staff displayed toward students

- clearly written aims and objectives

- a curriculum structure which ensured continuity and progression

- continuous pressure from the head to refine and extend practice.

In turn, the students were *visibly benefiting*, as was apparent from:

- their obvious pride in attending the school

- their desire to learn and to be successful

- the standard of their work

- the interest and confidence that they displayed

- their happiness, coupled with the fact that they were well-adjusted, socially and emotionally.

The majority of the students were judged to fulfil their academic potential.

As for the *contribution of the staff*:

- they were hardworking and dedicated

- everyone was working toward agreed common goals and in an atmosphere of mutual support

- they displayed a high level of professionalism at all times.

Other sources on which staff drew in order to justify their claims about the school's effectiveness included:

- the positive response of parents

- the favourable image of the school in the wider community

- the view of independent sources such as the HMI and LEA, eg, following a survey by HMI, the subsequent feedback by all account strongly underwrote what the school was attempting, praising fulsomely and voicing only minor criticisms

- the reaction of fellow professionals, eg, that other schools have adopted aspects of their practice

- the view of school governors, eg, that the school appeared to run very smoothly, with remarkably few problems of any magnitude.

Headteacher and management team

The headteacher emphasised that the school's effectiveness and success was due to team effort. Thus, whilst the management team exercised formal responsibility for determining whole school policy, the headteacher stressed that no major decision would be taken without all staff having been consulted and given an opportunity to air their views and concerns. He was a firm believer in delegation and empowering others — hence the organisational structure ie, the management team (described above), and at year level, a team of two (year leader and partner). The headteacher stressed the degree of autonomy colleagues enjoyed, though coupled with responsibility. Thus, for example, staff had a strong say in curriculum delivery and control over curriculum resources — both funds and learning materials.

There was a strong structure which all staff knew about and which it was intended should guide practice overall. It consisted of a broad framework, embracing:

- teamwork, based on the format of year leader and partner

- a system of topics which all teachers followed over a four year cycle.

Every member of staff was expected to subscribe to and operate within this framework. There was every indication that staff did so willingly.

> 'The most structured school I've ever been in ... I like it — you know where you stand.'
>
> *(Teacher)*

> 'It's structured and yet there's freedom.'
>
> *(Deputy Headteacher)*

The headteacher conceived of his leadership role in terms of helping to formulate the broad framework, and thereafter, to facilitate the capacity of the staff to translate the components of the framework into curriculum practice.

The headteacher won widespread acclaim from staff for the manner in which he led the school:

'I think he's a good leader because he sorts out what he wants to do, he rallies round his troops ... he delegates well, he's informed and enthusiastic — so you trust him, and he's very supportive.'

(Teacher)

'Effective management is best achieved by an informed manager who uses his skills to obtain the best overall results from his team by consultation, discussion and an understanding of the right time to achieve pre-determined *(sic)* goals.'

(Deputy Headteacher)

Additional factors to note about the managerial behaviour of the headteacher in particular, and to a lesser extent the deputy headteacher (central to whose role was providing pastoral care for the staff), included:

- a preparedness to provide explicit leadership, as necessary

- a determination not to allow his principles and broad objectives to be subverted or undermined by any member of staff

- a determination that the school should provide an education of the highest order for its students. Furthermore, that the school should be at the forefront of educational initiatives and practices. The head was perceived by staff to display a particular facility for timing:

  'You've got to be able to assess the time to move on, the time to consolidate, and to be able to 'read' people.'

- attaching particular emphasis to motivating staff and maintaining morale. He was widely regarded as genuinely caring for his staff. This helped to inspire staff loyalty:

  'His concern is his school, his children, his staff. We know he'll back us to the hilt.'

  (Teacher)

- attaching importance to good communications, making a point of being open with staff and ensuring that they were kept informed, but also encouraging and facilitating communication amongst staff

- making a point of having his finger on the pulse of the school. He employed a variety of means to achieve this, including: regularly getting around the school; taking on some teaching; and generally making himself accessible and approachable

- a concern to support members of staff and to facilitate their growth as autonomous professionals. In this regard emphasis was placed on accentuating the positive and remediating any shortcomings by indirect means, eg, giving over part of a professional training day to coverage of any areas of weakness and involving all staff

- exercising care when appointing new staff in an attempt to ensure that they would fit in with the existing staff. The relevant year leader's views would be sought in interviewing candidates, and all staff would have an opportunity to meet the candidates and would be consulted. The consequence of this is captured in the following comment by a teacher:

> 'Somehow or other he's got together a staff who really care about each other and who share a similar outlook.'

Furthermore, the head made it clear to any newcomer at interview that there was a system in place into which they would be expected to fit.

> 'If you come here, that's what you'll experience ... I'm not going to have someone come to us as a group and say ... I'm not going to accept this model (of operating).'

That said, there was a preparedness to consider new ideas which could be absorbed within the broad framework.

Vision, aims and strategic planning

The headteacher and staff had a clear vision of how and what they wished the school to be. The vision clearly had originated with the headteacher, who had taken steps to ensure that colleagues were aware of its component parts and fully behind it. Central to the vision was a concern for quality, this embracing holding high expectations of students and staff, together with the goal of continuous improvement.

> 'To aim for the highest standard that any child can achieve in a caring way, but not letting that caring interfere with that judgement ... You can make demands (of pupils) and (yet) you can care.'
>
> *(Headteacher)*

At the heart of the vision was the notion of the self-managing school and the self-managing teacher. The headteacher believed that the most effective motivation and commitment came from within a person rather than being enjoined on them — and for the simple reason that he or she had a direct stake in what was achieved overall. Hence his belief in trusting implicitly in colleagues' professionalism, affording them optimum autonomy although requiring accountability. Much was demanded of the staff who, in return, could expect to be fully supported.

This vision was communicated to staff by a variety of means:

- having things in writing

- making constant reference to it

- modelling for staff the qualities and values in which the head believed and which he wished to see reproduced

- using selected colleagues to reinforce the vision and assist its implementation.

This appeared to pay dividends, in that staff were well aware of what was at the core of the vision.

'He wants all his children to do the best they can.'

'He likes the staff ... to be knowledgeable ... to be well-informed, confident and self-managing ... able to sort out and look out for themselves, basically.'

The headteacher and fellow managers appeared to be thinking and planning strategically with respect to the school's future development. The headteacher was seen to anticipate likely future initiatives, to make a point of becoming fully informed about these, and to pass on this knowledge to his staff.

'He has the ability and the drive to foresee ... a great reader of trends to come ... He's a deep thinker ... It makes it easier for us to join on the conga line.'

(Deputy Headteacher)

'He never puts anything forward that he hasn't read thoroughly and thought through.'

(Teacher)

Further, he had the ability to prioritise, avoiding moving on too many fronts simultaneously. Consequently, it was widely felt that new initiatives frequently were taken up with the minimum of disruption — if indeed they were not already an integral part of existing practice!

Decision-making and communication

Policy decisions concerning whole school matters, including curriculum policy, in effect were taken by the headteacher in conjunction with other members of the management team. However, staff would have been consulted beforehand, both as a group and individually:

'Everyone is made to feel they contribute to decision-making.'

'We all feel that we are able to say what we feel. We can have our say.'

Although the process of decision-making was very open, nevertheless, by dint of personality the headteacher was able to wield a good deal of influence — not that he was seen to abuse his formal authority. Teachers referred repeatedly to the way in which they were left in no doubt as to what he wished to see happen, and to his powers of persuasion should the views of staff differ:

'You do get an influence, but if he's against it he'll do his best to persuade you round to his way ... Somehow or other he convinces you as to what he wants.'

However, once the broad decision had been taken, teachers enjoyed the freedom to decide how best to translate this into curriculum practice.

Communication appeared very sound at most levels in the school — a distinct advantage of the smaller school. That said, this was something on which the head set great store, going out of his way to keep colleagues fully informed of likely developments, and well in advance. He made extensive use of informal and personalised contact with individual members of staff, as well as of the more formal meeting with colleagues.

Professional relationships

The school was widely seen as go-ahead, and was an exciting place in which to work. The staff clearly derived satisfaction from this:

> 'Very much in the forefront of things, I would say ... and that gives you confidence.'
>
> *(Teacher)*

One of the staff employed the image of a journey aboard an express train to capture the feel of what it was like to work at the school:

> 'It's like being on a train. It's gathering speed ... faster and faster ... you come into a station and you do stop, but not for long before you're off again.'

Staff were worked hard by the headteacher, who was perceived as very demanding, but their effort and endeavour was continually being recognised and praised. Every one of them indicated that they felt that they were being extended professionally and that their expertise was being fully utilised. In addition, they had the reassurance of knowing that their head would support them 100%. The headteacher's confidence that here was a school in which was provided education of quality was seen to spread to staff:

> 'There's a sense of purpose in what people do ... they're confident and proud of what they're doing.'
>
> *(Headteacher)*

Without being complacent, the staff were aware of the quality of the school's practice:

> 'You're working hard and you're expecting to win things.'
>
> *(Deputy Headteacher)*

Again, this helped to boost self-confidence and to sustain morale. All in all, it meant that the workplace simultaneously was challenging, exciting and professionally rewarding.

There was every indication that professional working relationships in the school were very close and satisfying. Staff referred repeatedly to '*a team pulling together*' and '*team effort*'. They accorded each other mutual respect, and there was a readiness to support each other. Periodically, work spilled over into leisure activities:

> 'I think somehow or other he's got together a staff who really care about each other and who share a similar outlook.'

Other features of the school which helped to make it such a positive work environment included:

- that the school was well-organised

- that there were clear job descriptions for all

- that as teachers they had substantial classroom autonomy

- that the headteacher also worked hard, and more than played his part in the shared quest to maintain the school's success

- that no member of staff would be left to struggle if he or she was to experience pronounced difficulty in the classroom. There was a formal support structure involving, in the first instance, the year leader. No opprobrium was attached to asking for help. *'We're not afraid to say, – 'I'm really floundering here.'*

Monitoring and evaluation

This was regarded as fundamental to the quality of the education being provided by the school, and embraced both students and staff. The headteacher described how he monitored student progress by a variety of means, these including:

- regularly (daily) going in and out of classrooms and informally observing the school at work. He referred to this as 'managing by wandering around'

- requesting to see students' work on a systematic basis; also encouraging staff to send along students who had produced work of quality for credit stamping

- engaging directly in teaching (he had a teaching load of 0.4 approximately)

- carrying out or ensuring that particular areas of learning, notably, language, were tested periodically. He referred to this as 'the key to the curriculum'

- monitoring a number of other variables, eg, school attendance, the take-up of free school meals, the progress of students on the 'At Risk' register which Social Services maintained

- undertaking his share of playground supervision.

Relationships with governors, parents and the local education authority

Relations with the governing body, while sound, did not appear to be close or extensive. As a whole, the governors were reported by the headteacher and staff to have had little real influence to date, even in those areas for which they were now formally responsible. Thus, for example, staff remarked on the failure of some governors to see the school at work, and on their own lack of familiarity with the membership of the governing body. One member of staff, himself a teacher governor, noted:

> 'They're very supportive without interfering ... they're sympathetic, they back us up ... they're very rarely critical of what's going on.'

They were widely perceived still to look to the head for guidance, and to be more concerned with 'bricks and mortar' issues rather than educational policy. The teacher governor attributed this to the fact that the governors simply were out of their depth:

'You've almost got amateurs in a professional role.'

Attempts had been made to enhance the possibility of governors being able to contribute more substantially by, for example, assigning each governor to a particular year or area of the school. It seemed this had paid limited dividends to date however. There was confirmation from the vice-chair of the governing body of the limits of their role.

'We're here to oversee the management of the school but we're not the professionals, so we can't (cover) the educational side.'

In practice, typically, they had oversight of the school's general running, becoming involved with staffing issues, eg, hiring and firing, assisting the head in his struggle to restore the hours cut from SEN ancillary support, the physical fabric, budgetary matters, and exercising oversight of the implementation of the National Curriculum. While not disputing that they were constrained from being more fully involved in decisions about professional matters by their limited knowledge, the vice-chair referred to a simple shortage of time, which made it difficult to become better informed. Having a full time job, it was not easy to come in during school hours — a difficulty shared by some of her fellow governors.

Particular emphasis was attached by the headteacher to building and maintaining good relations with *parents*. They were made to feel welcome when on school premises, and were kept well-informed of any developments concerning their children. Staff claimed that they enjoyed an easy relationship with the majority of parents, who appeared content to leave educational matters to the professionals.

The school's relationship with the LEA was less close, it would seem mainly due to the physical distance from Shire Hall:

'We're the forgotten corner of _____, it's just the back of beyond.'

However, this did not appear to occasion any undue concern, on the part either of the headteacher or the staff. The former clearly delighted in exercising independence and individuality, and took pride in knowing that to a large extent they stood or fell by their own endeavours. The one exception to this was the 'patch' inspector for the school, who was described as *'super, very supportive'*.

EXAMPLE B: HEATHLANDS SCHOOL (*a pseudonym*)

School context

The school was a large voluntary aided, co-educational, comprehensive school and sixth form centre. The age range of the 1254 students was 11–19 and there were approximately 80 staff. The school was located in a predominantly rural area, had a large campus of approximately 22 acres and several buildings which had been erected since 1964, the most recent extension having been completed in 1990.

The management structure of the school comprised a senior management team (SMT) of the headteacher and two deputy headteachers; a senior management group of eight people (headteacher, deputy headteachers and five E allowance holders), and a larger school management group which included the middle managers (eg, heads of department and year), and which had an advisory rather than executive function. The school was organised on a departmental basis, and teachers were appointed as 'second in charge' in large departments or designated in charge of subjects, so that a large number of the staff had a formal managerial responsibility. The headteacher had been in post for seven years.

Perceptions of effectiveness

Every teacher interviewed thought that the school was effective in the work it undertook with students. The point that was made consistently was that it was effective for a wide range of students but was especially good with those of average ability. GCSE and A level examination results were cited to support these views. The only note of reservation, made by two teachers, was to query whether the school stretched its brightest students sufficiently. Teachers also spoke about the caring ethos of the school and the concern that was demonstrated for the students' personal and social as well as academic development. The headteacher identified the strengths of the school as:

> 'Its care for people; its concern for quality; its insistence on individual excellence; its recognition of individual achievement and fundamentally its belief that everyone has worth and a concentration therefore on people's strengths rather than an emphasis on weakness.'

The comments from the staff echoed this. The aspects of management that were referred to by various teachers and the Chair of the governors as indices of effectiveness were:

- that the school achieved its aims

- that all aspects of the school's work were carefully monitored and evaluated

- that the senior management team were proactive and tried to take people along with initiative

- that the governors and the parents had a voice in school decision-making

- that the staff as a whole were good at building a sense of community in the school.

Headteacher and management team

The headteacher and senior management team were regarded by the staff as a hardworking, close knit team who worked very effectively together. They were perceived as the key policy making group in the school, though major issues were discussed at the weekly meetings of the management group or more widely if this was required. The three members of the SMT were not always of one mind and the staff knew that they often had lively discussions about various policy options before deciding upon a course of action. One member of staff commented:

> 'The head doesn't manage alone but as the first among equals and that's good, because when they come out with a decision, I'm confident it has been discussed by a number of people who have different points of view.'

Another teacher speaking about what it was like to work in the school commented:

> 'It's very challenging, because the SMT lead by example and they like to be at the forefront of educational change; they work very hard but they expect you to work very hard and they set targets of what they expect the staff to do.'

The headteacher was widely perceived by the staff as someone who provided strong leadership, as being very open and honest, actively consulting staff and being prepared to adapt and change policies. One indicator of this open style was that the SMT had deliberately sought to create a balanced team in extending the management group to eight. They had tried to select people with complementary skills, and had included at least one person who they knew would be very challenging and would push them to question their assumptions. Comments made by teachers about the quality of leadership and management in the school were that it was:

> 'assertive, strong and supportive'
> 'effective, approachable and progressive'

One of the deputy headteachers observed:

> 'Management is about facilitating, creating an environment in which others can grow, take responsibility and be accountable.'

Additional factors to note about the managerial behaviour of the senior management team were that:

- they were good at motivating staff and students

- the headteacher was widely regarded as being loyal to the staff and inspired loyalty in return, individuals said that they were supported and helped with personal as well as professional problems

- the headteacher operated an open door policy, any member of staff could go and speak to him on any issue

- individual members of staff could put forward items for the agenda at a school management meeting

- many managerial tasks were delegated to the staff though always within a clear framework of accountability

- the management structure and processes, including job descriptions for deputy headteachers, heads of department, form tutors etc, were clearly set out and understood (they were included in the staff handbook)

- working parties were set up to explore particular issues (eg, communication)

- the day-to-day management of the school was generally stated to be very efficient.

Vision, aims and strategic planning

The headteacher and senior staff had a clear vision of the kind of place they wanted the school to be, and the broad components of this vision were known and understood by the staff. The school prospectus stated that the mission of the school was 'to provide a high quality education within the context of a Christian environment' and that a main aim was 'to develop the self-esteem, dignity and respect of all members of the community'. This vision combined a concern for caring and valuing individuals, as well as striving for quality, and this dual focus was not always easy to sustain. It was also a dynamic vision in that the headteacher recognised that the specific aims inevitably would alter over the years in the light of changing circumstances. This vision for the school was communicated to staff and students in a variety of ways:

- a statement of mission and aims was included in the school prospectus

- the staff handbook re-stated the importance of developing the school as a caring community eg, *Friendly staff interaction and support for one another are of major importance to the whole ethos of the school. It is people's strengths we want to maximise. When dealing with students we should always endeavour to maintain the self respect and dignity of the student.'*

- through encouraging staff to model caring behaviour and through the headteacher reinforcing the school's values when communicating with individuals or the whole school:

  'The message that I can get over and the way I want to say it is important for maintaining the ethos and philosophy of the school.'

  (Headteacher)

- by the headteacher and staff trying to ensure that the school policies and processes reinforced the school's underlying aims and values.

The headteacher and senior managers, and indeed managers at all levels in the school, appeared to be thinking and planning strategically about how the school should develop in the future. Several teachers commented that the SMT liked to be in the forefront of change and thought this could have advantages, (for example the introduction of the National Curriculum was relatively smooth, because the school had introduced a core curriculum in the late 1980s). The disadvantages were that the school was often trialling a range of different innovations and this increased pressure on the staff. One criticism that was levelled was that the senior staff possibly were too ready to implement government led innovations and not sure enough of their own convictions. In illustration, one member of staff said that though the school had been organised in mixed ability teaching groups for a number of years, and this had appeared to be a basic component of its philosophy, the introduction of national testing had given rise to proposals that streaming be reintroduced.

Decision-making and communication

Staff felt that the key decisions in the school were taken by the senior management team, though the wider senior management group of eight, which met on a weekly basis, was also seen as an influential body. Teachers in more junior positions could influence school policy through their head of department, by raising an agenda item at the school management meeting or by making their views known directly to the headteacher. However, several indicated that they felt their influence was rather limited and, although they were consulted, the consultation was often about how to do something rather than whether to do it. They recognised that they usually did not have either the information or the time to make a greater input. Individual teachers generally were more able to influence policy at departmental level. If there was a policy issue in the school on which opinion was known to be divided, the SMT had on a couple of occasions, arranged an open meeting in the evening to which all staff were invited so that the matter could be fully debated.

Communication at all levels in the school was felt to be good, especially between staff. However, one or two teachers thought it could still be improved in relation to students. Satisfaction in this area, which had been problematic, was generally attributed to a communications working party, as many of their suggestions had been implemented. Factors that staff said facilitated good communications were:

- the short morning briefings for staff (Monday, Wednesday, Friday — whole staff; Tuesday — departmental groups; Thursday — year groups)

- availability of 'post it' notes so that messages could be left in registers

- individual staff 'pigeon holes'

- agendas and minutes of meetings displayed in the staff room

- a notice board for students in each year group which gave them more independence

- the student journal as a means of communicating with parents

- regular newsletters for parents

- a comprehensive and up to date staff handbook

- a good induction programme for beginning teachers and teachers new to the school (including induction into office procedures from the bursar).

Professional relationships

Professional working relationships in the school were widely perceived to be good and many of the staff said that it was a happy and rewarding place in which to work. A majority of those interviewed felt that their expertise was being utilised and they felt valued as members of staff. They said that they were thanked for the work they did, and they received positive feedback, not just from the headteacher but from colleagues in their department, the head of department, a deputy headteacher etc. This increased their motivation and helped to make them feel good about themselves and the school. Several staff spoke of having to work hard and feeling pressured, but also said that the senior management team worked just as hard, if not harder. Positive features that were commented upon included:

- that individuals knew how the system worked and what they were supposed to do. The headteacher commented:

  'Everyone knows what's wanted, everyone knows what's expected and evaluation is a key factor of what we do.'

- every member of staff had an individual interview with the headteacher each year lasting approximately forty minutes. This was an opportunity to hear how he thought they were getting along and for them to say what they felt about working in the school, what their career aspirations were etc.

- staff were well-supported if there was any sort of disruption in the classroom; several staff said that it was a very safe school in which to work because back up support was available from a wide range of people, they were not blamed if they made a mistake, and they were not left to deal with problems on their own

- staff had autonomy in their work within a framework of accountability

- individual professional development was actively encouraged and supported through the INSET budget; the INSET funds were allocated to meet individual and departmental as well as whole school needs; the head and senior staff ran their own in-house training programme for middle managers and one for standard scale teachers was planned; role change and job/task rotation was practiced and encouraged.

Monitoring and evaluation

This was a key aspect of school management and it applied to both students and staff. Student progress was carefully monitored in a number of ways:

- a member of staff was appointed as academic tutor to each year group and moved up the school with the students

- every month each student was assessed on a simple check sheet in every subject. These sheets went to the head of department and the academic tutor

- the academic tutor was responsible for maintaining an overview of each student across the board, and if problems arose, working with the heads of department and the form tutors to take remedial action

- each student had a journal which was used as a homework diary and which had to be signed on a weekly basis by the form tutor and the parent; members of the SMT conducted regular spot checks to see the journals were kept up to date

- students who were judged not to be working well were called to the headteacher's office on a random basis during morning registration to have their homework checked by one of the SMT

- there was a clear disciplinary system which emphasised self-discipline and building good student/staff relationships and which had clear sanctions which teachers were asked to apply consistently

- the headteacher and deputy headteachers were on duty every lunch time in the dining room and in the grounds and used this as an opportunity to talk to the students and keep in touch with what was happening

- if a particular class was known to be causing problems for a teacher then one of the SMT would periodically call in at some point during the lesson to lend support to the teacher.

Monitoring and evaluation of the work of the staff was also carried on systematically. The headteacher's policy was to delegate managerial tasks but also to keep in touch with what was happening. He commented:

'I suppose part of my management style is the ad hoc, *how is this going?*'.

Day-to-day responsibility for monitoring the teachers' work rested with the heads of department and heads of year (who also acted as key stage co-ordinators for the national curriculum). The job description for heads of department specified that their foremost responsibility was 'to encourage, motivate and support all teachers of the subject'. Key ways in which teachers' work was monitored were:

- through the headteacher's annual meeting with each head of department when the examination results in that subject, the allocation of teachers to classes and the progress of staff in the department were on the agenda

- each of the deputy headteachers had been designated to oversee the work of a number of departments. They met each department head on a termly basis to discuss progress and any problems that had arisen

- the school conducted its own in-house evaluation. In the spring term each year each department was evaluated with a focus on a particular aspect that the SMT wished to explore across the school (eg, assessment). The evaluation had three broad components: visits to classes by the deputy headteacher responsible for the department and two or three other staff; a team led by the headteacher, and which might include a governor, which did pupil pursuits; and an interview by the deputy headteacher of teachers and the head of department — the whole exercise culminating in a written report for the department. The data from each department was used to compile a school report.

Relationships with governors, parents and the Local Education Authority

(363) Relationships with the governing body were stated to be good to excellent. The governors were reported by the Chair of the governing body, by the headteacher and by several of the staff to be a very committed group of individuals who worked hard for the school. They were perceived to have an impact on school policy and were not regarded as people who would automatically do what the headteacher suggested. However, the Chair of governors said that he could not think of a serious disagreement about policy between the headteacher and the governors which had stuck, commenting:

'So far we have always been able to come to a harmonious meeting of minds eventually, even if it has taken a few hours'.

The governors were involved in the management of the school through their work on various sub-committees, and many of them came into school regularly, met the staff and became involved in departmental evaluation exercises. They were perceived to be very supportive of the school, although a teacher governor felt that there was insufficient communication between the staff generally and the governors.

Relationships with the parents were also thought by the staff to be very strong in the school. The staff said that parents were made to feel welcome, efforts were made to communicate with them on a regular basis and their views were taken seriously. Indeed one member of staff suggested that the senior staff might be a little too sensitive to parental opinion! The school had a strong Parent Teacher Association which arranged many successful and well-supported functions, parents evenings were well-attended, and generally it was felt that parents were supportive of the staff and valued the school. One teacher commented:

> 'Relationships with parents, community and governors are an integral part of the whole working of the school and are very caring, constructive and rewarding.'

Because the school was a voluntary aided, denominational one, it had a very large catchment area and a particular definition of the community. The staff concept of the community was not the people who lived in the area around the school but rather the individuals and families in the students' home parishes. Links with these groups were strong and the senior staff worked to develop them. However, issues which impinged on the local community were not neglected. For example, a teacher reported that, one morning a week, at the headteacher's request, he spent some time before school in the bus station in a neighbouring town, keeping an eye on the behaviour of pupils as they boarded buses to take them to school. The school had received a complaint that students were rushing to get onto the bus before other passengers had got off and the teacher's presence was sufficient to calm the situation.

The school relationships with the LEA were also reported to be very positive. There appeared to be quite a strong link between the senior management team and the senior secondary adviser and between subject advisers and various departments, though these were more variable. The two deputy headteachers had been used as trainers on LEA run management INSET courses.

Comment

These two schools were perceived by their teachers and headteachers to be effectively managed. There was a close similarity in the features cited as evidence by staff in both institutions. What emerged was a picture of school management as a dynamic, interactive process, rather than a series of discrete tasks or techniques (eg, the budget, the timetable). Nor was it a responsibility for just a few people at the top of the school but something in which all staff were involved, albeit to varying degrees. These features were highlighted in both schools:

- There was a clear management structure, the school was well organised and there were written statements of the mission, aims and whole school policies.

- The management team had a clear vision for the school which the staff recognised and shared and which emphasised a concern for quality and individual excellence.

- The management team provided firm leadership but worked to empower staff and delegated many management tasks within a framework of accountability.

- Staff were involved in the decision-making process, were kept well informed about policy issues and the communication systems in the school worked effectively.

- The curriculum was sufficiently differentiated to meet the needs of the students and their progress was closely monitored.

- Staff had autonomy to plan and organise their own work but knew that they were accountable to management for their actions.

- Staff were able to work confidently because they knew that they could call on back-up support from management if it was required. Individuals were not left to cope with problems on their own.

- The management team worked hard and led by example, modelling the behaviours that they wished staff and students to emulate.

- The management team were proactive, constantly monitoring and evaluating school practice to see how it could be strengthened and improved. They also strived to keep the school abreast of developments in education locally and nationally.

- Professional working relationships between staff were good, they were used to working collaboratively and in teams. The school INSET programme was designed to meet whole school, group and individual needs.

- Relationships with the school governing body, the parents and the LEA were positive and strong (with the exception of the relationship between Waterfields School and its governors).

- The school climate was very open and staff felt able to express their views clearly. The school was notable for the genuine care that was displayed for staff. In turn, they felt valued and were happy working there.

Part 9

Summary, conclusions and implications

The purposes of this final Part are threefold:

1. to summarise the principal features and processes associated with the effective management of their schools, as perceived by the teachers and headteachers in the sample;

2. to draw together the main conclusions from the study and to relate them to relevant research findings from this country and abroad;

3. to identify some key implications for practice, policy and research.

In reading the following summary, several of the project's contextual features, including what it did and did not set out to achieve, should be borne in mind:

- this is an exploratory, descriptive study of a particular sample of well-managed schools, based upon the subjective, self-perceptions of the respondents, not a study of effective schools based upon objective, independent measures of outcomes

- the participating schools were self-nominated, not randomly selected, which inevitably produced a skewed sample of schools that are probably better managed than the average

- however, not all schools in the sample were necessarily well-managed in the eyes of all respondents, a fact which was evident from the questionnaire responses, particularly the open-ended comments

- the questionnaire and the interview schedule were designed on the basis of a review of the research literature, modified in the light of comments from the Steering Group and, as such, they represent a set of indicators, and an implicit model of effective management arrived at by a process of informed professional judgement

- the study focuses mainly on leadership and management structures and processes, rather than on technical and administrative tasks and skills (eg, those associated with timetabling or budgetary control), vitally important though the latter undoubtedly are

- a summary of the findings from a project of this type is bound to be over-simple and, at best, should be regarded as what the sociologist Max Weber called 'ideal typical' in that it seeks to capture the essence of a well-managed school. As such, it is unlikely to apply in its entirety to any one school and, thus, any generalisations have to be formulated with caution.

Summary and synthesis of main findings

The project's main aim was to identify management structures and processes in individual schools which staff in those schools have recognised as effective. Bearing all the foregoing caveats in mind, **the broad picture of effective management which emerges from this study is one which is remarkably similar for the 57 primary, secondary and special schools involved, indicating that some confidence can be placed in the findings.**

In what follows, we try to summarise the main features of well-managed schools, as perceived by the teachers and headteachers in our sample, using the indicators embodied in the questionnaire and the interview schedules. The summary is organised under headings similar to those used in the questionnaire and for this report. Some features come up under more than one heading because they interconnect with several aspects of school life: for example, the leadership styles of the headteacher and SMT influence both school ethos and decision-making, and several aspects of school ethos and professional relationships are similar to each other. Finally, **it is particularly important to recognise that what follows, in both the synthesis and the provisional model, are empirical findings from a particular sample of schools, not a set of recommendations about 'good' management practice,** though as indicated below, the majority of them are consistent with informed experience and the findings from earlier research.

Ethos

- Teaching and learning are given a high priority and there is a general concern to provide quality education. Complacency among staff is actively discouraged in favour of a questioning critical attitude and there is a continual striving for improvement.

- The teacher has high expectations of student behaviour and achievement and gives them the confidence to learn. Students play an active part in the life of the school and most of them experience a sense of achievement.

- The school provides good pastoral support for students and has established a relaxed but purposeful working atmosphere in which students and staff feel safe and secure.

- The headteacher and SMT hold high expectations of the staff, demand a lot from them but are sensitive to the teachers' workload and balance pressure and support.

- There is an open atmosphere in the school and a sense of community in which staff trust and respect one another and so feel able to talk freely about professional matters, to share experience and ideas and offer mutual support.

- The atmosphere is lively, there is a sense of change and activity which make it a stimulating, exciting and enjoyable place in which to work.

School 'outcomes'

- Staff perceive that: academic attainment is high; student attendance is consistently high; discipline is not a major problem; vandalism by students is not a major cause for concern; and most parents are proud that their children attend the school.

Aims

- The main aim in the school is to help each child achieve its potential by adopting a curriculum and teaching/learning style that are sufficiently differentiated to cater for individual needs.

- Meeting students' personal and social needs and promoting the acquisition of moral values are regarded by the staff as being as important as developing their academic potential, especially in primary schools.

- Providing a school environment in which students are happy, feel valued as individuals and learn to co-operate with one another.

Vison and school policy

- Staff are involved in developing the school's aims and policy, most of them understand and agree with the aims and policy and share a common set of educational values. Consequently, the staff have a shared sense of purpose.

- The school's aims and whole school policies are set down clearly in writing.

- The headteacher and staff have a clear vision about the school's future development and a plan about how to move in this direction. The 'vision' is constantly referred to and reviewed but is reasonably consistent over time and constant changes are avoided.

- The management team think and plan strategically and pay attention to school maintenance tasks as well as planning for development in the medium and longer term.

- The management team are proactive and keen to keep in the forefront of change. They are good at anticipating future developments and the implications these might have for the school.

- Management set out a broad strategy for change and support teachers during the implementation stage.

The headteacher

- Provides excellent leadership and a clear sense of direction; has a clear vision for the school based on beliefs and values; actively shapes the culture and ethos of the school; thinks and plans strategically; encourages quality and high expectations and discourages complacency.

- Has a consultative, 'listening' style; is decisive and forceful but not dictatorial; is open to other people's ideas; and is easily accessible to staff.

- Motivates staff; displays enthusiasm and optimism; is positive and constructive; often expresses appreciation to staff and celebrates special achievements.

- Models professional behaviour; does not stand on ceremony and is prepared to help out; takes ultimate responsibility and thereby makes staff feel secure; supports teachers in a crisis; protects staff from political or external interference; and is supported by the staff.

- Is well-organised; is in touch with events in the school; keeps abreast of new developments but avoids 'bandwagons'; prepares staff for future developments and avoids crisis management; strongly supports and regularly participates in staff and management development; and, especially in primary schools, has a structured annual dialogue with staff.

- Often communicates personally with pupils; is regularly seen around school; and is directly involved with pupils.

The headteacher and the senior management team

- Work well together as a team; have roles and responsibilities which are clear to staff; are highly visible and approachable.

- Take the key policy decisions but consult staff before doing so; face up to differences of opinion and work for a negotiated solution and a sense of joint ownership of school developments.

- Model desired behaviours and attributes (eg, hard work, commitment, mutual support and teamwork); behave with honesty and integrity in straightforward and non-devious ways; behave as if accountable to staff by providing clear evidence of the outcomes of their actions; are ready to admit mistakes and consider alternatives.

- Are good at 'people' management, including identifying and mobilising individual talents; regularly brief teachers about day-to-day issues; delegate meaningful tasks in order to develop and empower staff; monitor delegated tasks.

- Convey to staff a sense that the school is under control; support teachers' work in the classroom; provide good and consistent support to the staff; promote the school's image in the community.

Structure, decision-making and communication

- Teachers have easy access to school policy documents and staff handbooks, are regularly briefed by the SMT about day-to-day issues and generally feel well-informed.

- Staff meetings are used for discussion of major policy issues and working parties or small groups are used to investigate particular issues and make policy recommendations. Especially in primary schools, teachers feel they have a share in major decision-making.

- Meetings are usually well-chaired, purposeful and kept to a minimum.

- There is a clear organisational structure which is appropriate for meeting the school's aims and which is widely known and understood. A structure in which staff roles and responsibilities are defined, work loads are equitable, there are known lines of accountability and internal promotions are handled fairly. A structure which is sufficiently flexible that it can be altered to meet changing circumstances.

- Women deputies are not assigned traditional female responsibilities and, in primary schools, the proportion of women on the staff is reflected in the number of managerial positions held by women.

- In secondary schools, inter-departmental links are encouraged and both the departmental and the pastoral structures help the school to achieve its goals.

Professional working relationships

- There is a concern to build a learning environment; teachers strive to improve teaching and learning; they regularly discuss teaching methods in detail, engage in joint planning, prepare materials together and both seek and give advice.

- There is a good team spirit; staff are encouraged to co-operate with colleagues and are committed to working together; effective support structures are in place; new colleagues are made welcome and those in difficulty are supported.

- Staff feel valued; sensitivity is displayed to staff morale and feelings; teachers feel able to express their views openly and honestly; their contributions are given recognition in staff meetings, their views are taken seriously and they are encouraged to share experiences and successes.

- Professional development is an integral part of the job; management tasks are delegated to all levels and, as a result, teachers acquire new skills; most staff see their job as challenging but achievable; they feel happy and satisfied with their work; experimentation and reasonable risk taking are encouraged and staff are not penalised for failure but encouraged to learn from it; they are also encouraged to be involved in problem-solving on school-wide issues.

Links with parents and the community

- Staff work to build and maintain good relations with parents and there is an active and supportive PTA.

- Parents are made to feel welcome, are informed and consulted about significant developments affecting their children and are encouraged to ask about such developments. In primary schools, parents are encouraged to help in the classroom.

- Staff work to build and maintain community links and the school is responsive to the culture of the local community. In secondary schools, there are good links with local industry/commerce.

Governors and the Local Educational Authority

- Governors are ready to follow the headteacher's advice on most issues; staff and governors have a positive relationship. In secondary schools, governors play an important role in determining school policy.

- The relationship with the LEA is perceived to be generally sound rather than especially close or productive.

Managing change

- The school is receptive to innovation and change; the headteacher allocates money/resources for innovations; change is being successfully managed.

- The current reforms have led to an increase in collaborative decision-making which, while it takes more time, leads to better results and helps staff cope with stress.

- Effective use is made of the National Curriculum, school development plans, LMS, the devolved INSET budget, the five professional training days, school management training and open enrolment.

A provisional model

In general, the project's findings confirm that management is a highly complex, contingent and dynamic process which involves interactions between many people, in specific and diverse settings, in order to deal with tasks, roles, issues and problems which are themselves often complex and situationally specific. This complexity makes it essential that we first simplify the process in order to clarify and analyse it. Only then will we be in a position to understand it and, ideally, to indicate ways of helping managers to improve their performance. The foregoing summary and the following model are two means to those ends.

Figure 1 attempts to present the summary of the project's main findings in a provisional model of the key management features and processes in a well-managed school. The model has three, mutually interacting columns:

- Column 1: Contextual Factors

  This lists those factors which research and experience indicate have some considerable influence upon the school and its outcomes. Although our research did not deal directly with these influences, the open-ended questionnaire comments and the interview responses in the twelve schools frequently mentioned them, especially the impact of students' entry characteristics and parental support.

- Column 2: Internal School Management Features and Processes

  This is the core of the model and it is based directly on the project's research findings, as summarised above. Effective management is assumed to result from the interaction of the factors listed in the four boxes — 2A, 2B, 2C and 2D.

- Column 3: Outcomes and Feedback

  The factors listed here are also based directly on the research findings. Boxes 3A and 3B list some of what we may call intermediate outcomes related to the management of change — specifically the implementation of the current

Figure 1. Effective school management: a provisional model

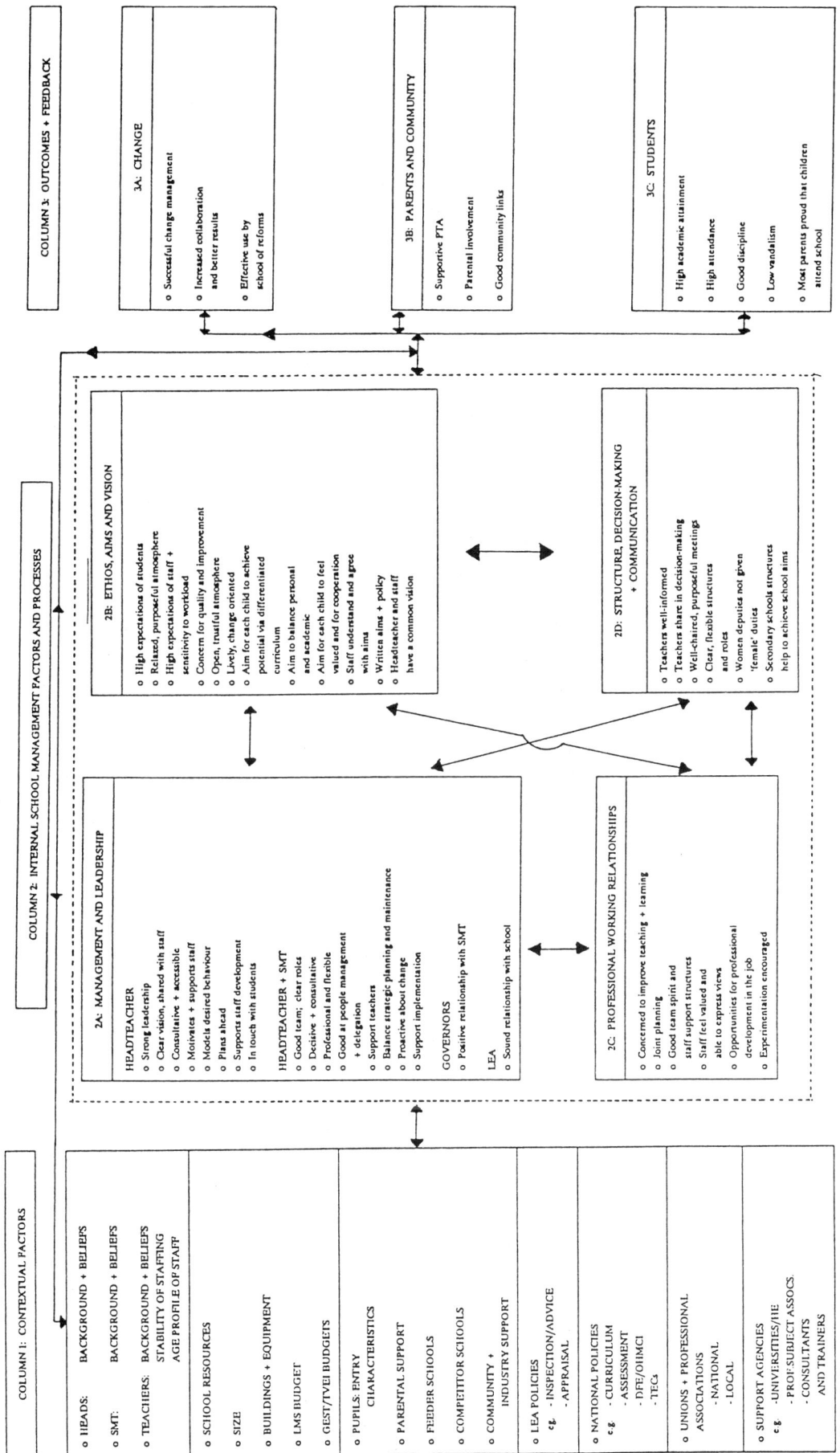

COLUMN 1: CONTEXTUAL FACTORS

o HEADS: BACKGROUND + BELIEFS

o SMT: BACKGROUND + BELIEFS

o TEACHERS: BACKGROUND + BELIEFS
STABILITY OF STAFFING
AGE PROFILE OF STAFF

o SCHOOL RESOURCES

o SIZE

o BUILDINGS + EQUIPMENT

o LMS BUDGET

o GEST/TVEI BUDGETS

o PUPILS: ENTRY
CHARACTERISTICS

o PARENTAL SUPPORT

o FEEDER SCHOOLS

o COMPETITOR SCHOOLS

o COMMUNITY +
INDUSTRY SUPPORT

o LEA POLICIES
e.g. - INSPECTION/ADVICE
- APPRAISAL

o NATIONAL POLICIES
e.g. - CURRICULUM
- ASSESSMENT
- DFE/OHMCI
- TECs

o UNIONS + PROFESSIONAL
ASSOCIATIONS
- NATIONAL
- LOCAL

o SUPPORT AGENCIES
e.g. - UNIVERSITIES/HE
- PROF/SUBJECT ASSOCS
- CONSULTANTS
AND TRAINERS

COLUMN 2: INTERNAL SCHOOL MANAGEMENT FACTORS AND PROCESSES

2A: MANAGEMENT AND LEADERSHIP

HEADTEACHER
o Strong leadership
o Clear vision, shared with staff
o Consultative + accessible
o Motivates + supports staff
o Models desired behaviour
o Plans ahead
o Supports staff development
o In touch with students

HEADTEACHER + SMT
o Good team; clear roles
o Decisive + consultative
o Professional and flexible
o Good at people management
+ delegation
o Support teachers
o Balance strategic planning and maintenance
o Proactive about change
o Support implementation

GOVERNORS
o Positive relationship with SMT

LEA
o Sound relationship with school

2B: ETHOS, AIMS AND VISION
o High expectations of students
o Relaxed, purposeful atmosphere
o High expectations of staff +
sensitivity to workload
o Concern for quality and improvement
o Open, trustful atmosphere
o Lively, change oriented
o Aim for each child to achieve
potential via differentiated
curriculum
o Aim to balance personal
and academic
o Aim for each child to feel
valued and for cooperation
o Staff understand and agree
with aims
o Written aims + policy
o Headteacher and staff
have a common vision

2C: PROFESSIONAL WORKING RELATIONSHIPS
o Concerned to improve teaching + learning
o Joint planning
o Good team spirit and
staff support structures
o Staff feel valued and
able to express views
o Opportunities for professional
development in the job
o Experimentation encouraged

2D: STRUCTURE, DECISION-MAKING + COMMUNICATION
o Teachers well-informed
o Teachers share in decision-making
o Well-chaired, purposeful meetings
o Clear, flexible structures
and roles
o Women deputies not given
'female' duties
o Secondary schools structures
help to achieve school aims

COLUMN 3: OUTCOMES + FEEDBACK

3A: CHANGE
o Successful change management
o Increased collaboration
and better results
o Effective use by
school of reforms

3B: PARENTS AND COMMUNITY
o Supportive PTA
o Parental involvement
o Good community links

3C: STUDENTS
o High academic attainment
o High attendance
o Good discipline
o Low vandalism
o Most parents proud that children
attend school

123

national reforms — and links with parents and the community. Box 3C lists the main student outcomes as perceived by the teachers and headteachers in the sample.

Two features of this model should be noted:

- No simple, left-to-right, causal relationships are implied and, in particular, no simple link should be inferred between columns 2 and 3 (eg, leadership and student outcomes). The model's main aim is to portray some of the complex interactions involved in school management and to generate further questions about the relationship of internal school management processes to the intermediate and student outcomes in boxes 3A, 3B and 3C (1) (footnote) and about the assumed feedback influence of the factors in column 3.

- It is only a provisional model, based on the empirical findings from a particular sample of 57 schools and **should not be interpreted as embodying recommendations about 'good' management practice** for all schools.

However, the model does a have some face validity and it is consistent with the conclusions from similar research in this country and elsewhere and could, therefore, serve as a framework to inform both school management training and future research. As such, it represents an interesting and potentially useful outcome from this exploratory study.

Conclusions

1. There was striking **agreement about the overall characteristics of well-managed schools** among staff in all types of school. This was the case in spite of the absence of data on student outcomes and the sometimes wide variations between several of the schools in the sample (as indicated in the quadrant analysis in Appendix 4). It is surely reasonable to conclude from this broad professional consensus that these findings are reasonably reliable and valid. The fact that, as we shall see below, they are consistent with findings from research elsewhere supports this interpretation.

2. Nevertheless, two overall differences are also noteworthy: first, there were statistically significant **differences between respondents in primary and secondary schools** on almost all the questionnaire items; second, the standard deviation for the responses from primary schools was consistently lower on most items than for secondary schools. It seems reasonable to conclude that there was greater agreement between teachers and headteachers in the sample of 33 primary schools (including a small number of middle and special schools) than between their counterparts in the 24 secondary schools that their schools were well-managed on the criteria used in the questionnaire.

The reasons for both findings could well be due to the different sizes of the two types of school. Primary schools have relatively small and simple structures which are probably relatively easy to co-ordinate, whereas secondary schools are relatively large, complex and less easy to co-ordinate at school level, but probably more tightly structured and easier to co-ordinate at departmental level. It may well be the case, therefore, that primary headteachers and teachers are more likely to have a shared understanding of the various aspects of school management than their secondary colleagues, whereas the latter are more likely to have that shared understanding at departmental level. There was some evidence that **subject departments** were the key management structures in secondary schools but there was little evidence of inter-departmental collaboration.

- Although relations between governors and staff in most of the sample of schools appeared to be positive, serious doubts were expressed in the schools visited, by governors as well as staff, about the **effectiveness of the governors** in contributing to the management of the schools. Across the whole sample, the governors' annual meeting for parents was not seen as influencing school policy.

- It was somewhat surprising to find that none of the respondents expressed any concern about using a term like **'management team'** in a primary school context and, more significantly, that team or collegial management appears to be emerging, and in some cases is well-established, in primary schools. This appears to reflect a substantial shift from the position of, say, ten years ago and may well be due to such factors as the increased scale and complexity of primary school management caused by the educational reforms, with the consequential need to share management responsibilities and, via the allowance system, to offer financial remuneration for managerial roles.

- The **importance of vision** in leadership was confirmed and reinforced by the interviews in the twelve schools. However, they also indicate the necessity for that vision to be more than a mere re-statement of the broad aims of British education: rather it must be thought through and spelled out in relation to the overall purposes and direction of a specific school. In addition, the findings indicate that the vision should, minimally, be communicated to staff in order that they might share it. It was further suggested that, ideally, it should be developed collaboratively with, and thus more easily shared by, the staff but there was little evidence of this happening in practice. Headteachers tended to develop their own vision for the school.

- Part of that vision should be to **create an open and positive school-wide climate or culture**. This was apparently easier in primary schools, which may be because of their smaller size and because the staff have broadly similar roles and tasks. The fact that most primary school staff are women may or may not be relevant.

- The arrangements for **decision-making, consultation and communication** were seen as crucial to the creation of that climate and to effective management. Most respondents appeared to want a combination of firm leadership and consultation over policy matters that directly affected their working lives. Most did not want to be consulted over detail but this varied between schools and between individuals. An important task for senior management is to recognise and act upon these distinctions. The value of using multiple means of communication, including networking, also emerged strongly.

- The importance of **consistency between espoused values and working realities** is also central to both vision and climate. Examples of this included the need for the headteacher and senior staff to model professional behaviour in their daily work, and for a school with an expressed commitment to equal opportunities to ensure that women and minority groups were appropriately represented in senior positions.

- Most respondents were committed to aims which stressed the **education of the whole child**. They did not regard 'to promote a spirit of competition' as a main aim of their school, clearly preferring 'to promote a spirit of co-operation' possibly because they interpreted both in relation to their classroom teaching, especially in primary schools. Respondents from primary schools also seemed to be much less comfortable than their secondary colleagues with the notion of academic aims but this may be simply a problem of terminology.

- The interviews in the twelve schools revealed that, although the respondents expressed definite views, giving clear explanations and reasons for them, about the **effectiveness of their school**, they did not appear to have a common professional language, frame of reference or criteria for describing and judging effectiveness. However, in all cases, it was recognised and accepted that the characteristics of the students on entry to the school and the quality of parental support which they received during their school career, had substantial impact on their performance and achievements.

- Most of the findings related to various aspects of the current **national reforms** indicated that they were mainly being implemented successfully, though with some difficulties and a certain degree of professional scepticism. In those cases (eg, national assessment, new forms of LEA inspections and teacher appraisal) where doubts were expressed about whether or not they were being effectively used by the school, this often reflected the fact that they were at an early stage of implementation and had not yet been experienced by the respondents.

Consistency with international research

The project's second and subsidiary aim was to identify international comparisons of management structures and processes which add to our understanding of effective practice. Both the summary and the model indicate that the project's research findings provide broad support for the eight propositions about the characteristics of effective school management, as generated from the international research literature and summarised in Section 1: strong purposive leadership by the headteacher; broad agreement between the headteacher and the staff on school goals, values, mission and policy; headteacher and deputies working as a coherent management team; teachers involved in decision-making on goals, values, mission and policy; a collaborative professional sub-culture; norms of continuous improvement for staff and students; leadership strategies which promote the maintenance and development of these and related features of a school's culture; and an enhanced capacity to implement reform.

In particular, it is encouraging to record the consistency of the project's findings with the ideas contained in the School Management Task Force Report (DES, 1990) which emphasises, inter alia, the importance of good leadership offering breadth of vision and the ability to motivate others; appropriate delegation with staff involvement in policy-making; clear purposes, goals and values shared by staff and reflected in the school's organisation and management; and a commitment to staff and management development. All of these find positive echoes in the project's findings.

The perceived centrality of the headteacher's role in the project schools is consistent with the findings from earlier research in this country (eg, Rutter et al, 1979; Mortimore et al, 1988; Nias et al, 1989). What comes through especially strongly from the present research is the need to take seriously the distinctions which are increasingly being made in the international literature between leadership and management. In brief, the term leadership is now being used to cover those aspects of the headteacher's role which are concerned with the mission, values and transformation of the organisation's culture or ethos, whereas management is used to cover the technical and administrative aspects. For example, Caldwell and Spinks (1992) using Sergiovanni's classification system say:

> 'There are many facets to the leadership role: technical, human, educational, symbolic and cultural, with the higher order symbolic and cultural facets being especially important...'

> '...In brief, technical leadership includes the capacity to plan, organise, co-ordinate and schedule. Human leadership involves the harnessing of available human resources in ways which include building and maintaining morale, encouraging growth and creativity, providing support for staff and empowering others in programs of development and through the creation of opportunities for participation in decision-making. Educational leadership involves the use of expert knowledge about education and schooling to diagnose students' needs, develop curriculum, select appropriate approaches to teaching and learning, supervise and evaluate. Symbolic leadership involves focusing the attention of others on matters of importance...through the range of words, actions and rewards...available to the leader. Cultural leadership involves the building of a strong school culture.'

Leithwood and Jantzi (1990) in an analysis of transformational leadership describe how leaders who display such behaviour help to:

> 'build shared meaning among...staff regarding their purposes and (create) high levels of commitment to the accomplishment of these purposes. Such leaders foster norms and beliefs among staff members about the contribution one's colleagues may make to one's practices. They also encourage openness to new ideas and practices...and careful assessment of such ideas and practices...Both individual and group reflection on purposes and practices and how they might be continuously improved are stimulated by the leader....'

More specifically, on the basis of a study of twelve schools which were perceived to have undergone substantial change, they identified six broad strategies which were employed to influence school cultures. Headteachers:

- strengthened the school's culture, eg, by clarifying and prioritising shared goals, by adopting measures to reduce teacher isolation

- employed a variety of bureaucratic mechanisms to stimulate and reinforce cultural change, eg, resources, decision-making structures, staffing procedures

- fostered staff development, eg, by providing resources for INSET, by initiating and/or delivering in-house training, by delegating power to others

- engaged in direct and frequent communication about cultural norms, values and beliefs

- shared power and responsibility with others, eg, by setting up working parties with a specific brief, by consulting widely

- used symbols to express cultural values, eg, by giving public recognition to teachers' achievements, by encouraging staff to share with colleagues ideas and practices.

The centrality of vision as an attribute of leadership is apparent in the international literature as well as in the current research.

However, though of undoubted value, there are potential dangers, most obviously in relation to the origin of the vision. The concept would appear to have been lifted from the commercial sector, where it has become associated with particular high profile businessmen and women. Thus, Beare, Caldwell and Millikan (1989) focused on the leader's role in formulating a vision when they reported that 'outstanding leaders have a vision for their organisation'. Caldwell and Spinks (1992) subsequently observed: 'This is unquestionably the finding of research, but it is a finding which is silent in respect to the manner in which the vision is generated.' While they acknowledged that there might be circumstances in which members of an organisation would look to the leader to provide the vision, as advocates of the self-managing school, their preference was for the vision to be formulated by leaders and others together.

A similar line was taken by Sergiovanni (1991), who cautioned about the idea of vision commencing with a single person or, alternatively, being created by a committee. While noting the responsibility of headteachers to talk openly about their beliefs, principles and commitments, and to encourage a dialogue about what the school stands for and where it should be headed, he stressed that vision should not be construed as a strategic plan upon which was charted precisely what to do. Fullan too (1992) articulated the dangers of visions being too bound up with a given individual and being pursued too narrowly and slavishly. Headteachers:

'are blinded by their own vision when they feel they must manipulate the teachers and the school culture to conform to it. Such a vision does not serve long-term development. 'My vision', 'my teachers', 'my school' are proprietary claims and attitudes which suggest an ownership of the school that is personal rather than collective, imposed rather than earned, and hierarchical rather than democratic.'

The evidence from the rapidly expanding literature on transformational leadership strongly underscores the point that if the vision is to serve an effective function it needs to be attainable, must be made explicit and public, taken onboard and lived — that is, experienced. Research from various professional arenas has underlined the importance of involving a range of people in decision-making in accordance with individuals' expertise and allowing for the fact that not all teachers will wish to be involved in all decisions. To enable this to happen staff will need to be provided with opportunities to acquire relevant knowledge and skills. Finally, Caldwell and Spinks address the style of leadership that is appropriate to the self-managing school.

'The dominant principle of organisation has shifted, from management in order to control an enterprise to leadership in order to bring about the best in people and to respond quickly to change ... it is a democratic yet demanding leadership that respects people and encourages self-management, autonomous teams, and entrepreneurial units.'

Some implications

1. School management

Although the project did not set out to produce recommendations for action, the findings presented in this report do have two important characteristics: they have face validity, in that they reflect the situation in 57 schools, and they are consistent with research and experience both here and abroad. Thus, headteachers and others with school management responsibilities should be able to adapt the practical findings embodied in the report itself, in the summary and in the provisional model to their own situations with some confidence.

The concept of the self-managing school is now widely accepted as the way forward, and most commentators see it as including such key components as strategic leadership, collaborative decision-making with teachers and governors and accountability. The findings from this study certainly speak to these issues.

2. Management training and development

For similar reasons, those concerned with management training and development should be able to make practical use of the findings. Notwithstanding the need for further research and development work, as outlined below, the 'map' of practical knowledge which is now available as a result of this and earlier work enables us to outline with considerable confidence what kind of knowledge and skills effective school leaders should have. The complexity of effective school management and its inherently contingent nature have been stressed and should underlie any development programme. But the vitally important contribution of such factors as leadership, vision, culture, collaborative decision-making and the like should surely figure prominently in training and development activities, including the projected mentoring schemes for new headteachers. They should also inform the on-the-job development programmes and appraisal schemes within each school and LEA. The findings should also be taken into account in the formulation of competences for headteachers and other school managers.

The findings relating to the role of governors pose problems of a different order, including some for policy makers, as indicated below. As far as trainers are concerned, they point to the need to address directly the weaknesses and deficiencies identified in this report. One way of tackling them might be to adopt the Swedish approach and run more joint training for governors, headteachers and senior staff.

3. Research and development

The project has thrown up the need for a follow-up **development project aimed at school improvement**. Although the questionnaire and the interview schedule were designed for research purposes, they could be adapted and re-designed as a diagnostic tool to assist schools to engage in self-review and improvement. This diagnostic tool would focus on, and seek to improve, management processes and structures, with the ultimate aim of improving the school's overall effectiveness. In order to produce a reliable and effective diagnostic tool, it would probably be necessary to mount a short development project to re-design the existing instruments and trial them with a group of primary and secondary schools. The outcome would be a diagnostic tool, together with some suggestions for its use, which could then be made available to schools and trainers.

The project's findings also highlight the need for a follow-up **research study on effective management for effective schools**. The present project is an exploratory, descriptive one based on teachers' and headteachers' perceptions of effective management in a sample of self-nominated schools. It has produced rich and instructive data with considerable practical import. The fact that the Z scores produced some wide variations between several of the schools in the sample (see the quadrant analysis in Appendix 4), supports the view that the instruments were using criteria which tap important aspects of effective school management and, hence, increases the likelihood that they and the findings are valid. The next step would be to use this experience to inform a second study to try to establish the relationship between management processes and student outcomes. This would involve a design based upon a random sample of schools (ie, including both well-managed and less well-managed ones) and the collection of 'hard' outcome data like SATS, examination results (eg, GCSE, A-levels and NVQs), truancy rates and students' 'destinations', together with data about school management processes collected via a refined version of the instruments used in the present study and a management audit. As part of such a project, the role and impact of management processes in subject departments in secondary schools, which are increasingly being recognised as important (Reynolds and Cuttance, 1992), could also be studied. The outcome would be an important contribution to our practical knowledge about the effective management of effective schools.

4. Policy

The project also raises some important policy issues for consideration at national and local levels. For example, assuming that the above suggestions for management development and training programmes are accepted, then the implications for training supported under the school management activity within the Grants for Education Support and Training (GEST) programme should be considered. Similarly, if the suggestions about using the findings as the basis for management competences are accepted, then the implications for the appraisal of headteachers and other school managers and for the criteria to be used in the new arrangements for the inspection of schools should be seriously considered.

The finding that teachers in the sample of schools tended to judge effectiveness in terms of their own somewhat subjective and school-specific criteria should be taken into account as policies on school inspection and the use of objective measures of school performance are formulated and implemented. So, too, should their conviction, which is strongly supported by research evidence (2), that the character of the school's catchment area and other external factors significantly influence student performance and other school outcomes. It is clear that, vitally important though school management and leadership undoubtedly are in improving the effectiveness of schools, their contribution is necessarily constrained by factors outside their control.

The findings relating to the roles and effectiveness of governors in school management are disquieting but are consistent with other, impressionistic evidence. They suggest the need for a detailed and specific review of policy and practice in this area.

5. The Profession

Finally, the project raises some important professional issues and implications. British headteachers and teachers are facing, and will continue to face, challenging and turbulent times. The pace and scale of the current, national reforms are without precedent in this, and arguably any other, country: American and European educationalists, for example, find it difficult to grasp the extent of the changes and re-structuring taking place here. Under such circumstances, it is remarkable that the teachers and headteachers in our sample of schools were managing the implementation of these changes so successfully and that they were so co-operative in this project.

In addition to such massive changes as the National Curriculum and national testing, industrial style techniques like appraisal and competence-based training and the introduction of a quasi or social market with an emphasis on diversity of provision and customer choice, headteachers and teachers are now responsible, together with the governors, for the local management of schools. The short-hand term for this is the self-managing school. The long-term question is: what kind of school leaders, managers and teachers are needed to ensure that such self-managing schools are effective? It is apparent from the project's findings that the traditional, autonomous and sometimes autocratic approach to headship is quite inappropriate. As far as our respondents are concerned, effective management involves a clear vision, collaboratively arrived at, and shared, by the staff; an open school culture in which professional collaboration is at a premium; conditions of work which encourage active reflection, professional scrutiny of teaching and the possibility of learning in and on the job because it is both challenging and achievable; an acceptance of professional accountability; and strong, purposeful leadership which encourages a commitment to student learning and continuing school improvement.

Implicit in this list is the certainty that personal and professional values lie at the heart of educational leadership in the self-managing school and, ultimately, this is a perspective which raises fundamental questions about the nature of educational leadership in a democracy. The implications for the qualifications, selection, induction and continuing professional education of headteachers and senior staff, as well as teachers as a whole, are, therefore, far-reaching. This is a challenging and daunting agenda for the profession and for those responsible for its governance, including any putative General Teaching Council.

Notes

1.   The data were not collected in a form suited to a satisfactory correlational study and although an exploratory factor analysis and a series of regression analyses were carried out, they simply confirmed that a new and different study would be required to research these issues.

2.   Relevant research evidence is helpfully summarised in Reynolds and Cuttance, 1992.

References

Barth, R (1986) 'Principal-centered professional development' *Theory into Practice* 25.3 pp 156-160

Beare H, Caldwell B J and Millikan R H (1989) *Creating an Excellent School: Some New Management Techniques* London: Routledge

Blase D W and Kirby J (1992) *Bringing Out the Best in Teachers* Newbury Park, California: Corwin Press

Bolam R (1990) 'The management and development of staff' in Saran R and Trafford, V (eds) *Research in Education Management and Policy: Retrospect and Prospect* Lewes: The Falmer Press

Caldwell B J and Spinks J M (1992) *Leading The Self-Managing School* Lewes: Falmer Press

Campbell P and Southworth G (1990) *Rethinking Collegiality: Teachers' Views* A paper presented at the AERA annual conference, Boston, Massachusetts, April. Cambridge: Cambridge Institute of Education

Coulson A A (1986) 'The managerial work of primary school headteachers' *Sheffield Polytechnic Papers in Educational Management* No. 48 Sheffield: The Polytechnic

Daresh J (1988) *The Preservice Preparation of American Educational Administrators: Retrospect and Prospect* Paper presented at the British Educational Management and Administration Society (BEMAS). Greeley: University of Northern Colorado

Deal T and Peterson K (1990) *The Principal's Role in Shaping School Culture* Washington, DC: USDE/OERI

Department of Education and Science (1990) *Developing School Management: The Way Forward. A report by the School Management Task Force* London: HMSO

Duke D (1986) 'The Aesthetics of Leadership' *Educational Administration Quarterly* Vol.22, No.1

Duttweiler P C (1990) 'A broader definition of effective schools' in Sergiovanni T J and Moore, J H (eds) *Target 2000: A Compact for Excellence in Texas's Schools* Austin, Tx: Texas Association for Supervision and Curriculum Development

Fullan M (1992) Visions That Blind *Educational Leadership* 49. 5. pp.19-20

Fullan M and Steigelbauer S (1991) *The New Meaning of Educational Change* (2nd ed) London: Cassell

Hargreaves A (1992) 'Cultures of Teaching: A focus for change' in Hargreaves A and Fullan, M (ed) *Understanding Teacher Development* London: Cassell

Hopes C (ed) (1986) *The School Leader and School Improvement: Case Studies from Ten OECD Countries* Leuven, Belgium: ACCO/OECD

Hoyle E (1986) *The Politics of School Management* London: Hodder and Stoughton

Leithwood K A (1992) The Move Toward Transformational Leadership *Educational Leadership* 49. 5. pp.8–12

Leithwood K, et al (1990) The Nature, Course and Consequences of Principals' Practices *Journal of Education & Administration* 28. 4. pp.5–31

Leithwood K and Jantzi D (1990) *Transformational Leadership: How Principals Can Help Reform School Culture* A paper presented at the AERA annual conference, April. Toronto: The Ontario Institute for Studies in Education, Centre for Leadership Development

Levine D U and Lezotte L W (1990) *Unusually Effective Schools: a Review and Analysis of Research and Practice* Madison WI: National Center for Effective School Research and Development

Lightfoot S L (1983) *The Good High School* New York: Basic Books

Lipsitz J (1984) *Successful Schools for Young Adolescents* New Brunswick, NJ: Transaction

Little J W (1982) Norms of Collegiality and experimentation: workplace conditions of school success *American Educational Research Journal* 19.3 pp 325–340

Little J W (1990) 'Teachers as Colleagues' in Lieberman A (ed) *Schools as Collaborative Cultures* Basingstoke: Falmer Press

Morgan G (1991) *Riding the Waves of Change* San Francisco: Jossey Bass

Mortimore P, et al (1988) *School Matters: The Junior Years* Salisbury: Open Books

Nias J (1989) *Primary Teachers Talking: A Study of Teaching as Work* London: Routledge

Nias J, Southworth G and Yeomans R (1989) *Staff Relations in the Primary School* London: Cassell

Owens R G (1970) *Organisational Behaviour in Schools* New York: Prentice Hall

Peters T (1987) *Thriving on Chaos* London: Macmillan

Reynolds D and Cuttance P (eds) (1992) *School Effectiveness: Research Policy and Practice* London: Cassell

Rosenholtz, S J (1989) *Teachers' Workplace: the Social Organization of Schools* New York: Longman

Rutter, M, et al (1979) *Fifteen Thousand Hours* London: Open Books

Schein E H (1989) *Organizational Culture and Leadership* San Francisco: Jossey-Bass

Seashore-Louis K and Miles M B (1990) *Improving the Urban High School: What Works and Why* New York: Teachers College Press

Sergiovanni T J (1991) *The Principal* (2nd ed) Boston: Allyn and Bacon

Sergiovanni, T J and Starrat R J (1983) *Supervision: Human Perspectives* New York: McGraw Hill

Snyder K J, et al (1992) A Tool Kit for Managing Productive Schools *Educational Leadership* 49. 5. pp. 76-80

Weindling R and Earley, P (1987) *Secondary Headship: the First Years* Windsor: NFER/Nelson

Yeomans R (1987) 'Leading the Team, Belonging to the Group' in: Southworth, G (ed) *Readings in Primary School Management* Lewes: Falmer Press

Appendices

Appendix 1

The Steering Committee

The Steering Committee met on nine occasions between February 1991 and July 1992. The members of the Committee are listed below.

AMMA	Meryl Thompson
NAIEA	Michael Jolley
NASUWT	Sue Rogers
NAHT	Jeff Holman
NUT	Michael Barber
PAT	David Jones
SEO	Geoffrey Williams
SHA	Brian Stevens
SMTF	Alan Evans
DFE	Robert Mace
DFE	Pauline Leonard

Appendix 2

Invitation for Schools to participate in The Project

The Schools participating in the project were identified through the teacher associations. The six associations (AMMA, NAHT, NASUWT, NUT, PAT, SHA) each placed a notice in their journal or bulletin inviting teachers and headteachers to nominate their school to participate in the project. The broad shape and content of the advertisements were agreed by the association representatives in advance. The notice placed by AMMA in Issue 42 of its UPDATE (January, 1991) is reproduced below as an example.

Is your school a standard bearer?

How are schools managing to provide high quality education despite the pressures of recent legislation? What can schools do to improve? Commentators — often people who have not set foot in a school for a considerable time — have essayed their own answers to these questions, but AMMA, acting in concert with the other teachers' associations, thinks the profession itself is best placed to suggest some useful pointers.

A Professional Working Party of the School Management Task Force is looking at how schools have addressed the key management tasks of the last three years — which is where **you** come in.

The Task Force, which draws members from the education and business worlds, was set up by the Government, and its report **Developing School Management — The Way Forward** will already be familiar to many members. All the teachers' associations are represented on the Professional Working Party.

Do you feel that your school has maintained, or improved, its high quality of education since the implementation of recent legislation? Does the system of management make a significant contribution to achieving these standards? If so, AMMA would like to include your school in the Professional Working Party's research programme designed to demonstrate examples of successful management.

Schools which respond will be asked to complete a questionnaire, and some may be visited at a later stage in the research. Examples and advice on good practice will be published, but the schools involved will not be identified.

All the teachers' associations are urging their members to take part, and the Working Party believes the most useful responses will come from schools where there has been a good measure of staff involvement in the decision to contribute.

If you have views to express, please write to Meryl Thompson at AMMA Headquarters quoting the reference **Developing schools**, including details of your school and a brief account of how it has managed the recent changes. We would appreciate it if there could be just one response per school.

Appendix 3

Effective Management in School's Project

NDC EMP

National Development Centre for Educational Management and Policy
School of Education, 35 Berkeley Square, Bristol BS8 1JA. Tel. 0272 303030 Ext. M283.

Effective Management in Schools

A Joint NDC/CREATE Project: Funded by the DES Task Force
and Supported by the Teacher Associations in the Professional Working Party
(AMMA; NAHT; NASUWT; NUT; PAT; SHA)

TEACHERS' QUESTIONNAIRE

The aim of this study is to identify examples of management structures and processes in individual schools which staff of these schools have recognised as effective practice.

The investigation has two main phases:

o   the present questionnaire survey to obtain heads' and teachers' views;

o   case studies in a selection of schools using interviews with heads and staff to explore the issues in more depth.

The purpose of this questionnaire is to obtain your perceptions and views on various aspects of management in the school. It forms a major part of the project and the information you give will enable us to establish a clear picture of teachers' views of school management.

Please answer every question. The first section of the questionnaire seeks basic factual information where answers should be written in or circled to indicate the appropriate response.

The rest of the questionnaire has been designed as a series of statements where your agreement/disagreement can be indicated by circling the appropriate number. Space is provided at the end of each section for you to add further comments or explanation.

Please answer each question by circling the number which most closely represents your opinion using the following 5 point scale:

5   SA = Strongly Agree
4   A = Agree
3   DK = Don't Know
2   D = Disagree
1   SD = Strongly Disagree

Please make a reasonably quick and general response giving your overall judgement about the various aspects of effective management in _your_ school.

We would stress that all the information you provide will be treated in the strictest confidence.

Please return the questionnaire in a sealed envelope to the person who gave it to you by **April 22nd.**

UNIVERSITY OF BRISTOL

Telex 445938 BSUNIV-G   Fax (0272) 251537

141

EFFECTIVE MANAGEMENT IN SCHOOLS PROJECT

TEACHERS' QUESTIONNAIRE

Name of school: ....

How many years have you been in teaching? ....

How many years have you been at this school? ....

How many schools, including this one, have you worked in? ....

Are you Male or Female?   Male/Female

What post or incentive allowance do you hold? Standard scale/A/B/C/D/E/Deputy Head

What areas of responsibility, if any, do you hold?   None/Please give details

What is your main teaching subject/specialist age range? ....

....

A. SCHOOL ETHOS, AIMS AND POLICY

Please Circle

1. **In this school:**

	SA	A	DK	D	SD	Card 1.
o most pupils feel a sense of achievement	5	4	3	2	1	42
o academic attainment is high	5	4	3	2	1	43
o teachers give pupils the confidence to learn	5	4	3	2	1	44
o good pastoral support is provided for pupils	5	4	3	2	1	45
o discipline is not a major problem	5	4	3	2	1	46
o vandalism by pupils is not a major cause for concern	5	4	3	2	1	47
o the buildings and grounds are well maintained	5	4	3	2	1	48
o staff and pupils feel safe and secure	5	4	3	2	1	49
o there is a relaxed but purposeful working atmosphere	5	4	3	2	1	50
o pupil attendance is consistently high	5	4	3	2	1	51
o teachers have high expectations of pupil achievement	5	4	3	2	1	52
o teachers have high expectations of pupil behaviour	5	4	3	2	1	53
o pupils play an active part in the life of the school	5	4	3	2	1	54

2. **In this school:**

	SA	A	DK	D	SD	
o a main aim is to achieve good academic results	5	4	3	2	1	55
o a main aim is to meet personal and social needs	5	4	3	2	1	56
o a main aim is to promote the acquisition of basic skills	5	4	3	2	1	57
o a main aim is to promote the acquisition of religious values	5	4	3	2	1	58
o a main aim is to promote the acquisition of moral values	5	4	3	2	1	59
o a main aim is to promote a spirit of cooperation	5	4	3	2	1	60
o a main aim is to promote a spirit of competition	5	4	3	2	1	61
o a main aim is to help each child to achieve its potential	5	4	3	2	1	62

3. **In this school:**

	SA	A	DK	D	SD	
o most staff understand the school's aims and policy	5	4	3	2	1	63
o most staff agree with the aims and policy	5	4	3	2	1	64
o staff are involved in developing the school's aims and policy	5	4	3	2	1	65
o most staff have a shared sense of purpose	5	4	3	2	1	66
o most staff share a common set of educational values	5	4	3	2	1	67
o the school development plan is used to review the extent to which aims have been achieved	5	4	3	2	1	68
o there is an explicit equal opportunities policy and this is generally implemented	5	4	3	2	1	69
o there is a concern to build a learning environment for staff as well as pupils	5	4	3	2	1	70

4. **What are your views and opinions on the school's ethos, aims and policy?**

71

143

B. LEADERSHIP AND MANAGEMENT

Please circle

1. **The headteacher:**

		SA	A	DK	D	SD	
o	provides a clear sense of direction for staff	5	4	3	2	1	5
o	is regularly seen around the school	5	4	3	2	1	6
o	is directly involved with pupils	5	4	3	2	1	7
o	is easily accessible to staff	5	4	3	2	1	8
o	is open to other people's ideas and suggestions	5	4	3	2	1	9
o	provides excellent leadership for the school	5	4	3	2	1	10
o	effectively promotes the school in dealings with the community at large	5	4	3	2	1	11
o	strongly promotes staff development activities	5	4	3	2	1	12
o	strongly promotes management development activities	5	4	3	2	1	13
o	often communicates personally with individual staff to express appreciation for special effort	5	4	3	2	1	14
o	regularly participates in staff development activities	5	4	3	2	1	15
o	has a structured dialogue with each member of staff at least once a year	5	4	3	2	1	16
o	can be relied upon to support the teachers in a crisis	5	4	3	2	1	17
o	often communicates personally with pupils to praise special effort	5	4	3	2	1	18

2. **The headteacher and deputy/senior management team:**

o	work well together as a team	5	4	3	2	1	19
o	take the key policy decisions	5	4	3	2	1	20
o	consult staff before reaching major decisions	5	4	3	2	1	21
o	provide good and consistent support for the staff	5	4	3	2	1	22
o	promote the school image effectively in the community	5	4	3	2	1	23

3. **What are your views and opinions on the quality of leadership and management in the school?**

24

144

C. STRUCTURE, DECISION MAKING AND COMMUNICATION

Please circle

SA A DK D SD

1. **In this school:**

		SA	A	DK	D	SD	
o	the staff have clear job descriptions	5	4	3	2	1	25
o	incentive allowances appear to be mainly awarded to teachers for managerial responsibilities	5	4	3	2	1	26
o	the current incentive structure helps in the achievement of the school's aims and policy	5	4	3	2	1	27
o	women deputy headteachers are not assigned traditional female responsibilities	5	4	3	2	1	28
o	the proportion of women in the staff is reflected in the number of managerial positions held by women	5	4	3	2	1	29
o	the proportion of teachers from ethnic minority groups in the staff is reflected in the number of managerial positions that they hold	5	4	3	2	1	30

Card 2.

2. **In this school:**

		SA	A	DK	D	SD	
o	staff meetings are used for discussion about major policy issues	5	4	3	2	1	31
o	teachers generally feel well informed	5	4	3	2	1	32
o	working parties or small groups are used to investigate particular issues and to make policy recommendations	5	4	3	2	1	33
o	teachers are regularly briefed by the senior management team about day to day issues and news	5	4	3	2	1	34
o	teachers are clear about the different roles and responsibilities of each member of the senior management team	5	4	3	2	1	35
o	each teacher has easy access to school policy documents and staff handbooks	5	4	3	2	1	36
o	teachers feel that they have a share in major decision-making	5	4	3	2	1	37
o	teachers are ready to accept the responsibility which goes with shared decision making	5	4	3	2	1	38
o	meetings are kept to a minimum	5	4	3	2	1	39
o	meetings are usually purposeful	5	4	3	2	1	40
o	meetings are usually well chaired	5	4	3	2	1	41

3. **What are your views and opinions on the effectiveness of the structure, decision making and communication procedures in this school?**

42

D. THE COMMUNITY, GOVERNORS AND THE LEA

1. **In this school:** **Please circle**

		SA	A	DK	D	SD	Card 2.
o	staff work very hard to build and maintain good relations with parents	5	4	3	2	1	43
o	staff work hard to build and maintain close relationships with the wider community	5	4	3	2	1	44
o	parents are always made to feel welcome	5	4	3	2	1	45
o	parents are informed and consulted about significant developments bearing on pupils	5	4	3	2	1	46
o	parents are encouraged to ask questions about educational practice	5	4	3	2	1	47
o	parents are encouraged to help in the classroom	5	4	3	2	1	48
o	there is an active and supportive parent-teacher association	5	4	3	2	1	49
o	parent evenings are well attended	5	4	3	2	1	50
o	most parents are proud that their children attend the school	5	4	3	2	1	51
o	our activities are responsive to the character and culture of the local community	5	4	3	2	1	52
o	staff play an active role in the community	5	4	3	2	1	53
o	pupils play an active role in the community	5	4	3	2	1	54
o	members of the community play an active role	5	4	3	2	1	55
o	there are good links with local industry/commerce	5	4	3	2	1	56
o	there are good links with local community organisations	5	4	3	2	1	57

2. **In this school:**

		SA	A	DK	D	SD	
o	the staff and governors have a positive relationship	5	4	3	2	1	58
o	the governors play an important role in determining school policy	5	4	3	2	1	59
o	the governors are ready to follow the head's advice on most issues	5	4	3	2	1	60
o	the governors' annual meeting for parents is a valuable influence on school policy	5	4	3	2	1	61
o	there is a close and productive relationship with the LEA	5	4	3	2	1	62
o	ideas about improving existing practice are freely exchanged with colleagues from other schools	5	4	3	2	1	63

3. **What are your views and opinions on relationships with the parents, the community, governors, the LEA and other schools?**

64

E. **PROFESSIONAL WORKING RELATIONSHIPS**

Please circle

SA A DK D SD

1. **In this school, teachers:**

		SA A DK D SD	
o	feel able to express their views openly and honestly	5 4 3 2 1	5
o	feel that their views are taken seriously by management	5 4 3 2 1	6
o	are encouraged to be involved in seeking solutions to problems facing the school	5 4 3 2 1	7
o	go out of their way to make new colleagues feel welcome and at ease	5 4 3 2 1	8
o	are encouraged by the head and senior staff to cooperate with colleagues on joint activities	5 4 3 2 1	9
o	are committed to working together as much as possible	5 4 3 2 1	10
o	regularly discuss teaching methods and approaches in some detail	5 4 3 2 1	11
o	regularly engage in joint planning of new approaches to teaching and learning	5 4 3 2 1	12
o	often prepare teaching materials together	5 4 3 2 1	13
o	often seek and give each other practical advice about classroom teaching	5 4 3 2 1	14
o	often observe each other teaching and give constructive feedback	5 4 3 2 1	15
o	experiencing difficulties receive support from their colleagues	5 4 3 2 1	16
o	are constantly striving to improve teaching and learning	5 4 3 2 1	17
o	have developed effective strategies for record-keeping	5 4 3 2 1	18

2. **In this school:**

		SA A DK D SD	
o	there is a good team spirit among the staff	5 4 3 2 1	19
o	staff support the headteachers	5 4 3 2 1	20
o	management tasks are delegated to staff at all levels	5 4 3 2 1	21
o	teachers develop new skills by undertaking delegated management tasks	5 4 3 2 1	22
o	teachers feel happy and satisfied with their work	5 4 3 2 1	23
o	teachers feel that senior managers support their work in the classroom	5 4 3 2 1	24
o	staff contributions and achievements are given public recognition in staff meetings and on similar occasions	5 4 3 2 1	25
o	staff are encouraged by the head to share their experiences and successes	5 4 3 2 1	26
o	most staff see their job as challenging	5 4 3 2 1	27
o	most staff see their job as achievable	5 4 3 2 1	28
o	professional development occurs as an integral part of the job as well as through INSET courses	5 4 3 2 1	29

3. **What are your views and opinions on professional working relationships in this school?**

30

F.   MANAGING CHANGE   **Please circle**

1.   **In this school:**   SA A DK D SD

		SA	A	DK	D	SD	
o	the current reforms have led to increased collaborative work among the staff	5	4	3	2	1	31
o	collaborative decision making about the implementation of change takes more time but leads to better results	5	4	3	2	1	32
o	collaborative ways of working help staff to cope with stress	5	4	3	2	1	33
o	the head ensures that, wherever possible, money and resources are allocated to support the planning and implementation of innovations	5	4	3	2	1	34
o	we are coping well with the introduction of the national curriculum	5	4	3	2	1	35
o	we are very receptive to innovation and change	5	4	3	2	1	36
o	change has been successfully managed in this school	5	4	3	2	1	37
o	we are coping well with the introduction of national assessment arrangements	5	4	3	2	1	38

2.   **The school is making effective use of the following initiatives:**

		SA	A	DK	D	SD	
o	LMS	5	4	3	2	1	39
o	school development plans	5	4	3	2	1	40
o	the five professional training days	5	4	3	2	1	41
o	the devolved INSET budget	5	4	3	2	1	42
o	appraisal of teachers and headteachers	5	4	3	2	1	43
o	the national curriculum	5	4	3	2	1	44
o	national assessment	5	4	3	2	1	45
o	open enrolment	5	4	3	2	1	46
o	governors' new powers and responsibilities	5	4	3	2	1	47
o	LEA inspections	5	4	3	2	1	48
o	school management training	5	4	3	2	1	49

3.   **What impact have these developments had on the management of the school?**   50

4.   **What features of the school's management system have most influenced its ability to cope and develop as an institution in the last 3-5 years?**   51

5.   **What are your views and opinions about how these changes have been managed?**   52

G. SECONDARY SCHOOLS ONLY

Please circle

SA S DK D SD

1. In this school: Card 3.

    o   inter-departmental links are encouraged   5 4 3 2 1   53
    o   the departmental (or faculty) structure helps
          in the achievement of the school's aims
          and policy   5 4 3 2 1   54
    o   the house/year/upper and lower schools structure
          helps in the achievement of the school's aims and
          policy   5 4 3 2 1   55
    o   the pastoral and academic aspects of the curriculum
          are well integrated   5 4 3 2 1   56
    o   pastoral and academic staff roles are well
          integrated   5 4 3 2 1   57
    o   one main aim is to prepare school leavers for the
          world of work   5 4 3 2 1   58

H. ALL SCHOOLS

1. **Please set out any further views and opinions on issues related to the effective
    management of your school.**   59

Thank you for taking the time to complete this questionnaire. Please seal it in the envelope provided and return it to your school contact person as soon as possible and not later than Monday, 22nd April, 1991.

EFFECTIVE MANAGEMENT IN SCHOOLS PROJECT

PRIMARY

HEADTEACHERS' QUESTIONNAIRE

Card 1.

Name of School: 5–6

LEA: 7

Name: 0

Are you Male or Female?   Male/Female 8

Type of School: e.g.Infant, Junior, JM & I, Middle, 11-16, 11-18, VI form college:

.... 9

Mixed or single sex? 10

Age range of pupils: 11

Status of school: Maintained/Voluntary Aided/Grant Maintained/Voluntary Controlled 12

Current number of pupils on roll: 13–16

Total number of Teachers (NOT including the Head)
          Full-time: ....Part-Time:...............Total FTE:................... 17–24

Is the catchment area of the school: Inner City/Mainly Urban/Mainly Rural/Rural and Urban 25

How many sites does the school operate on? 26

How many years have you been Headteacher at this school? 27–28

Were you appointed head from inside or outside the school?   From Inside/From Outside 29

How many headships, including this one, have you held? 30

How many years have you been in teaching? 31–32

Have you got a fully delegated budget?   YES/NO 33

If not, when will this be introduced? 34

ALL SCHOOLS EXCEPT SECONDARY

What is your approximate teaching load?   0.2   0.4   0.6   0.8   1.0 35

How much secretarial support do you have, approximately?   0.2   0.4   0.6   0.8   1.0 36

Please explain any key organisational or structural features of the school, including the way in which incentive allowances are linked to tasks and responsibilities.

37

EFFECTIVE MANAGEMENT IN SCHOOLS PROJECT

SECONDARY

HEADTEACHERS' QUESTIONNAIRE

Card 1.

Name of School: 5-6

LEA: 7

Name: 0

Are you Male or Female?   Male/Female 8

Type of School: e.g.Infant, Junior, JM & I, Middle, 11-16, 11-18, VI form college:

.... 9

Mixed or single sex? 10

Age range of pupils: 11

Status of school: Maintained/Voluntary Aided/Grant Maintained/Voluntary Controlled 12

Current number of pupils on roll: 13-16

Total number of Teachers (NOT including the Head)
         Full-time: ....Part-Time:...............Total FTE:.................. 17-24

Is the catchment area of the school: Inner City/Mainly Urban/Mainly Rural/Rural and Urban 25

How many sites does the school operate on? 26

How many years have you been Headteacher at this school? 27-28

Were you appointed head from inside or outside the school?   From Inside/From Outside 29

How many headships, including this one, have you held? 30

How many years have you been in teaching? 31-32

Have you got a fully delegated budget?   YES/NO 33

If not, when will this be introduced? 34

SECONDARY SCHOOLS ONLY

How is your school structured? Please tick those which apply.

House system	35
Year system	36
Upper/Middle/Lower schools	37
Subject departments	38
Faculty system	39
Other	40

Please comment/explain	
	41

Appendix 4

School average Z scores for output and process measures: Primary

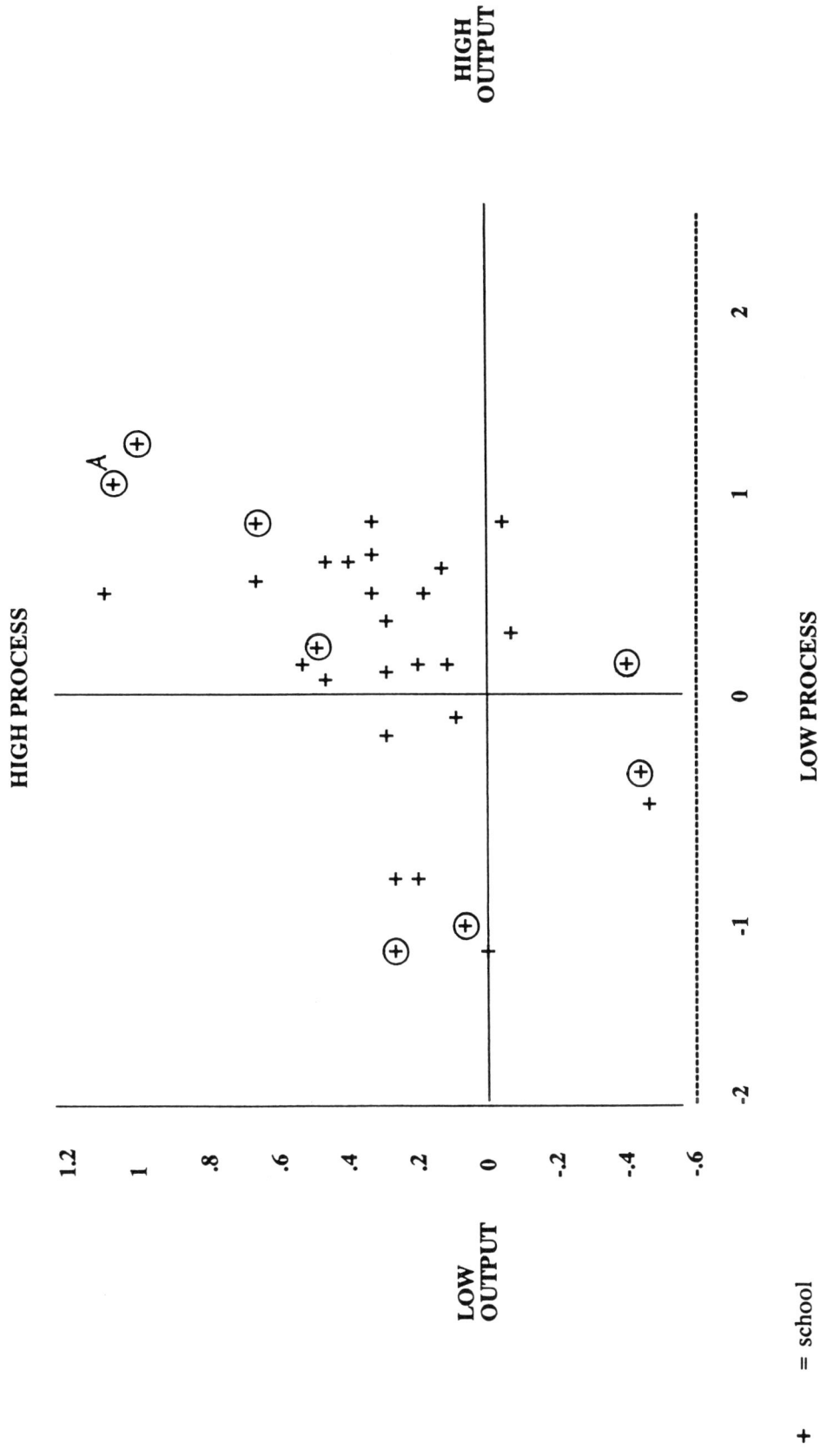

+ = school

⊕ = school visited

⊕A = school described in Section 8

153

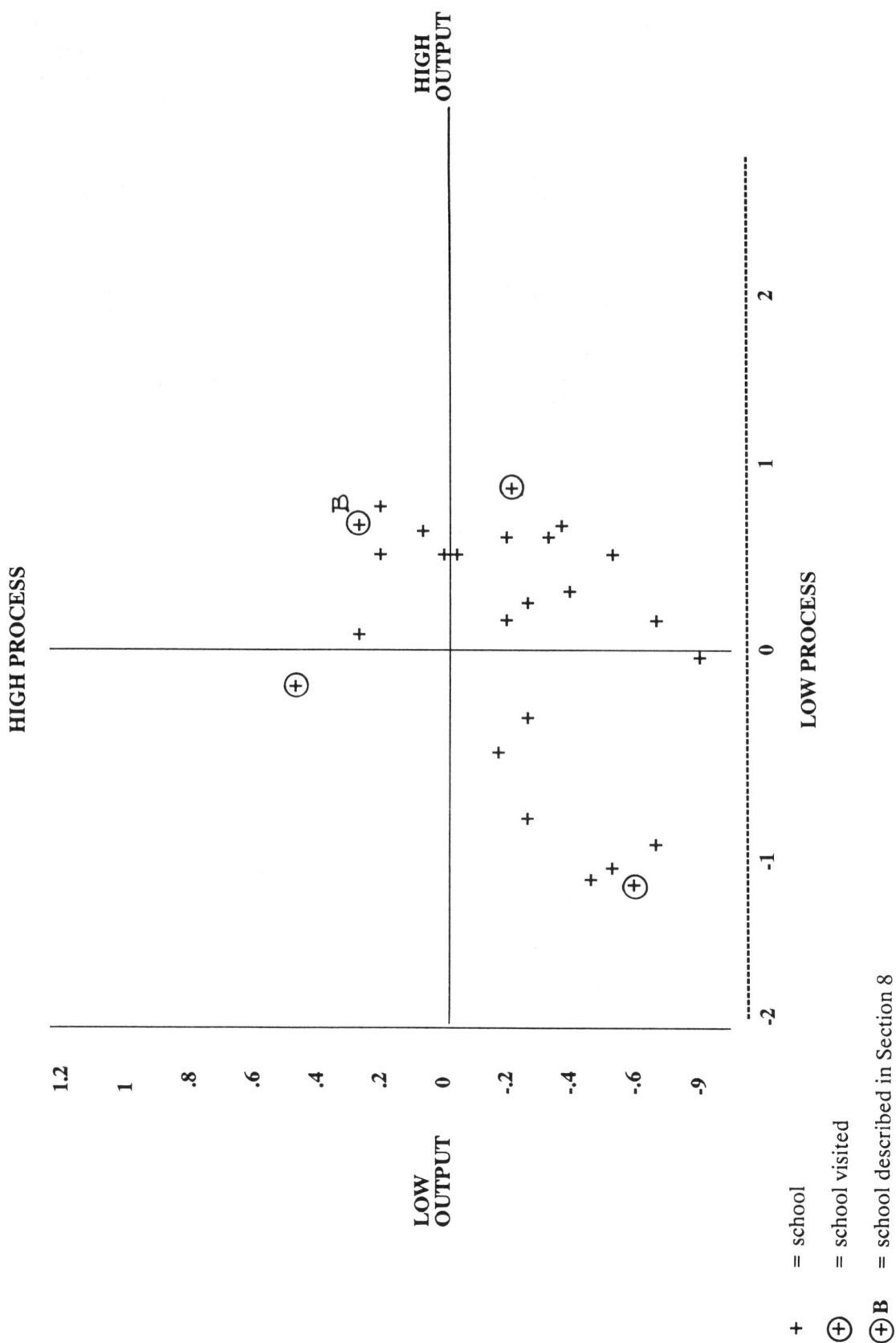

School average Z scores for output and process measures: Secondary

154

Appendix 5

Return rates of questionnaires

Numbers	Headteachers			Teachers			Headteachers + Teachers		
	Received	Expected	%	Received	Expected	%	Received	Expected	%
Primary (includes special, middle)	33	33	100	218	276	80	251	309	81.2
Secondary	24	24	100	368	432	85	392	456	86
Total	57	57	100	586	708	82.8	643	765	84

Types of school in sample (N = 57)

1. Primary

Nursery/Infants	5
Junior	8
Primary (JMI)	15
Middle	1
First	2
Special	2
	33

2. Secondary

11–16	6
11–18	17
6th Form College	1
	24

3. School Size

Smallest	56 students
Largest	1,500 students

Headteachers in survey (N = 57)

1. Gender

	Primary	Secondary	Special	Totals
Male	17	20	1	**38**
Female	14	4	1	**19**
Total	31	24	2	**57**

2. Number of headships

No. headships	Percentage
1	56
2	37
3	3.5
4	3.5

3. Whether appointed from inside/outside school

	N	%
From within school	12	21
From outside	45	49

Teachers + headteachers (N = 643)

1. Gender

Male	39.3%
Female	60.7%

2. Years at school

1 year	21%
2	13
3	10
4	7
5	6
6	4
7–10	13
11–15	11
16–20	8
20+ years	7

3. Catchment of Schools

Inner city	14%
Mainly urban	47
Mainly rural	16
Rural + Urban	23

1. Posts held by teachers/headteachers

Post	Number	Percentage
Standard Scale	225	25.8
A	74	11.8
B	108	17.2
C	39	6.2
D	57	9.1
E	21	3.3
Deputy headteacher	47	7.5
Headteacher	57	9.1
Total	628	100

(Missing Data 15)

2. Number of schools worked in (teachers only)

No of schools	No of teachers	Percentage
1	140	24.2
2	142	24.5
3	112	19.3
4	86	14.9
5	43	7.4
6	20	3.5
7	17	2.9
8	9	1.6
9+	10	1.7

(Missing Data 7 Teachers)

Basic features of the twelve site-visit schools

School	No. of children	F.T.E (excluding H.T.) No. of teachers	Headteacher		
			Yrs at the school	Sex	No of h/Ships
1	160	6	4	Female	1
2	196	9	1	Female	2
3	245	8	13	Male	3
4	c.300	12	4	Female	2
5	328	13	1	Male	1
6	475	18	12	Male	2
7	280	14	14	Male	2
8	1,420	87	3.5	Male	1
9	1,000	59	4	Female	1
10	1,202	73	6	Male	1
11	1,100	66	9.5	Male	2
12	178	25	1.3	Male	2

Interviews conducted in twelve schools

	Headteachers	Deputy Headteachers	Teachers	Governors	Total
Primary	7	6	28	6	47
Secondary	4	4	31	4	43
Special	1	1	4	1	7
Totals	12	11	63	11	97

Appendix 6

Interview schedule for headteachers

A. SCHOOL ETHOS, AIMS AND POLICY

1   Can you describe for me what it is like to work in this school?

2   People often use metaphors to capture succinctly complex ideas and situations.
    Does a suitable metaphor spring to mind which would characterise your school?

3   Do you consider this to be an effective school?
    If so, in what respects?

   Probes: What do you consider to be the school's main strengths?
                 What do you consider to be the school's greatest weaknesses?

4   Do you have a vision of what you want this school to be in, say three to five year's from now?

   i   Please describe this to me.

   ii   How did you arrive at this?

   iii   Are the staff aware of this vision?
         If so, how did this come about (eg, documents, discussion, etc,)?

   iv   To what extent do staff share this vision?

B. LEADERSHIP AND MANAGEMENT

5   How would you describe your style of leadership?

6   On which aspects of your role as head do you place priority?

7   From what you know or have heard, what are the main similarities and differences between your approach to management and that of your predecessor?

8   How do you keep your finger on the pulse of the school?

9   As a manager, what do you consider to be your strengths and weaknesses?

10 **Primary only:**   i   Is there a recognisable senior management (team) at this school?

    All   ii   Do senior managers work well together as a team?

    All   iii   Have you got the right balance of personalities and expertise/skills in the team?

11 In relation to how the school is managed, what do you consider are the main strengths and weaknesses?

C. STRUCTURE, DECISION MAKING AND COMMUNICATION

12 i   How are policy decisions arrived at in the school?

Probe: Do people other than yourself contribute to policy-making?

ii   Do you consider there is sufficient consultation of staff prior to policy decisions being made?

13 Do marked differences of opinion arise with regard to policy matters? If so, how, typically, is such a situation handled?

14 Are you intending to make any (further) changes to the way that the school is structured and organised?

D. PROFESSIONAL WORKING RELATIONSHIPS

15 i   What are the main areas over which staff have considerable autonomy?

ii   To what extent do you delegate?

Probe: Having delegated, look for evidence of follow through.

16 To what extent do the staff work together collaboratively?

17 i   How much emphasis is placed on the continuing professional development of members of staff?

ii   How do you actually set about promoting/facilitating this?

18 What happens at your school if there is a teacher whom everybody knows is not doing very well?

19 How open or guarded are you in what you say and to whom?

20 Informal customs and rituals often develop in schools. Can you think of any such customs/rituals which exist in your own school?

21 What evidence do you have of (active) collegiality among school staff?

E. MANAGING CHANGE

22 What strategies do you employ to assist the process of change and development?

23 With regard to your vision for the school about which you spoke earlier:

i   How close do you consider you are to realising this?

ii   What measures/steps are needed in order to move things forward decisively?

iii   What do you see as the single greatest obstacle to attaining your vision?

F. THE COMMUNITY, GOVERNORS AND THE LOCAL EDUCATION AUTHORITY

24 What is the school's standing in the local community?

25 Are you and colleagues seeking to project a particular image of the school upon the local community?
If so, please describe this.

26 i   How, if at all, have the following contributed to the management of the school?

(a) Governors
(b) Parents
(c) LEA officers and inspectors

ii   How significant a contribution do you consider this to have been?

Interview schedule for staff members

A. SCHOOL ETHOS, AIMS AND POLICY

1   Can you describe for me what it is like to work in this school.

2   People often use metaphors to capture succinctly complex ideas and situations.
    Does a suitable metaphor spring to mind which would characterise your school?

3   Do you consider this to be an effective school?
    If so, in what respects?

4   i   Does the head have a vision for the school?
         If so, can you describe this for me?

    ii   How did you learn about it?

    iii Did you play a part in shaping this vision?

    iv   To what extent do you and your colleagues share this vision?

B. LEADERSHIP AND MANAGEMENT

5   i   How would you describe your head's style of management?

    ii   Do you consider your head to be a good leader?

6   From what you know or have heard, what are the main similarities and differences between the present head's approach to management and that of his/her predecessor?

10 **Primary:**   i   Is there a recognisable management team at this school?

   All   ii   How well do you consider the head and senior managers work as a team?

8   In relation to how the school is managed, what do you think are the main strengths and weaknesses?

C. STRUCTURE, DECISION MAKING AND COMMUNICATION

9   i   How are policy decisions made in the school?

    ii   Do you have the opportunity to contribute to policy-making?
         If so, in what way/by what means?

    iii Would you like to have a greater say?

10 How effective do you consider channels of communication in the school to be?

11 Are you aware of marked differences of opinion having arisen in relation to matters of school policy?
If so, how were these situations dealt with/resolved?

12 Can you think of any changes in the way that the school is structured or organised which, if implemented, could increase its effectiveness?

D. PROFESSIONAL WORKING RELATIONSHIPS

13 i   What are the main areas over which you have considerable autonomy?

   ii   To what extent would you say the head delegates?

14 i   Do you feel that your expertise is being fully utilised at the present time?

   ii   Do you feel valued as a member of the staff?

15 Are there opportunities to work collaboratively with colleagues or do you mainly work separately?

16 How far are you encouraged to experiment and try things out, and to work out your own solutions to problems which arise?

17 To what extent do you talk informally about professional matters with your colleagues?

18 How open or guarded are you in what you say and to whom?

19 i   Are you encouraged to think about your continuing professional development?

   ii   To what extent are you actively supported in this?

20 What happens at your school if there is a teacher whom everybody knows is not doing very well?

21 Schools often develop informal customs and rituals. Can you think of any such customs/rituals which exist in your own school?

E. MANAGING CHANGE

22 i   How would you like to see this school develop over, say, the next 3–5 years?

   ii   What do you think would need to be done in order to achieve this?

23 In your opinion, how well is change managed in this school?

24 i   With regard to moving the school forward substantially, what measures do you consider are needed?

   ii   What do you see as the single greatest obstacle to the further substantial development of the school?

F. THE COMMUNITY, GOVERNORS AND THE LOCAL EDUCATION AUTHORITY

25 What is the school's standing in the local community?

26 i How, if at all, have the following contributed to the management of the school?

(a) Governors
(b) Parents
(c) LEA Officers and inspectors

ii How significant a contribution do you consider this to have been?

Interview schedule for governors

BACKGROUND

1 How long have you been a governor of this school?

2 For how long have you been Chair of Governors?

A. SCHOOL ETHOS, AIMS AND POLICY

3 Can you describe for me what this school is like?

People often employ metaphors to capture succinctly complex ideas. Does a suitable metaphor spring to mind which would characterise this school?

4 Do you consider this to be an effective school?
If so, in what respects?

Probes: What do you consider to be the school's main strengths?
What do you consider to be the school's greatest weaknesses?

5 i Do you think that the head has a vision for the school?
If so, can you describe this for me?

ii Did you or any of the governing body play a part in shaping this vision?

iii How is the governing body involved in the management of the school?

B. LEADERSHIP AND MANAGEMENT

6 How would you describe the head's style of leadership?

7 From what you know or have heard, what are the main similarities and differences between the present head and his/her predecessor in their approach to management?

8 i How effective a leader do you consider the head to be?

ii What would you say are his/her main strengths and shortcomings?

9 How well do you consider the head and senior staff work together as a team?

10 In relation to how the school is managed, what do you think are the main strengths and weaknesses?

E. MANAGING CHANGE

11 What do you consider to be the most significant change, for better or worse, that has taken place in the school over, say, the past three-years?

12 In your opinion how well is change managed in this school?

F. THE COMMUNITY, GOVERNORS AND THE LOCAL EDUCATION AUTHORITY

13 What is the school's standing in the local community?

14 How much community involvement is there in the school?

15 What are the relations like between the school and the governors?

16 How influential do you consider the governors have been in shaping school policy?

17 Has there been any marked disagreement between the head and the governing body over any aspect of school policy or practice?

18 What are the relations like between the LEA and the school?

19 How significant do you consider has been the contribution of the LEA to the management of the school?

Printed in the United Kingdom for HMSO
Dd 0295649 C20 5/93 531/3 12521